A TASTE OF
NATURE ISLAND COOKING

THE CUISINE OF DOMINICA

●

Hyacinth I.R. Elwin

CARIBBEAN

First published 1998 by
MACMILLAN EDUCATION LTD
London and Basingstoke,
Companies and representatives throughout the world

ISBN 0–333–71970–0

10   9   8   7   6   5   4   3   2   1
07   06   05   04   03   02   01   00   99   98

This book is printed on paper suitable for recycling and
made from fully managed and sustained forest sources.

Printed in Hong Kong

A catalogue record for this book is available from the
British Library.

Illustrations by Loye Barnard and Sylvia Duckworth

Cover illustrations by Loye Barnard

To the memory of
my mother, Da,
who encouraged me.
And to
my father and
grandmother
who were the cooks in the family.

Contents

Foreword

From a very early age, one of my life's ambitions was to compile into book-form the local recipes of my country together with our unique cooking methods and eating habits.

The opportunity for me to pursue this ambition came in 1974 when, as a student of the Caribbean Regional Youth Development Centre: Commonwealth Youth Programme, I researched and compiled a number of recipes which had been prepared over the years by Dominicans.

However, the motivating factor which prompted me to carry out this study was the realisation that many of these recipes were being forgotten. Modernisation and development were, to an extent, eroding the use, as well as the method of preparation, of our indigenous foods. The need to preserve this aspect of our culture for the benefit of future generations was a further incentive to pursue this study.

It is a truism that the surest way of knowing a country and its people is to study their eating habits, the food they eat, the way they cook it, when and why. This collection records some of the well-loved recipes developed in Dominica as a result of both historical and sociological influences, presenting the reader with some insight and flashing glimpses of what makes up Dominicans.

Hyacinth Elwin
12 August 1998

Preface

Dominica's traditional cuisine, like its history, folklore and language, is a reflection of Creole mixture and adaptation since the period of cultural contact between the indigenous Caribs and the peoples of Africa and Europe. In recent years, the island's history has been studied through documentary research, through dance forms and through linguistics. Now, Hyacinth Elwin has provided us with another form by which to understand the ingredients of our island culture and to savour the multiplicity of influences on our lifestyle. She has chosen food – that most vital of our needs – as a method of tracing the historical record, and in doing so has compiled a detailed collection of Dominican recipes.

Miss Elwin has spent the better part of her working life involved in social work and welfare in Dominica. She pioneered special programmes for youth from the 1960s. She has served in the Girl Guides and promoted 4-H groups and church organisations as the building blocks of community development. To list the numerous programmes with which she has been associated over the years would take up too much space here, but the thread which links them all has been her concern for improved nutrition through community education. She has shown how, with a little imagination and the sharing of skills, the profuse variety of nutritious fruits and vegetables in Dominica can be transformed into wholesome and tasty dishes.

As her work took her to villages all over Dominica, Miss Elwin's years of endeavour in this field also exposed her to numerous methods of food preparation, ranging from the processing of cassava in the Carib villages to the sauces and stews of the more French-influenced communities on the north and south-east coasts. Her experiences took her across class as well as space from the small farmer's 'one-pot-hold-all' to the more elaborate fare served from the traditional oven and *potagé* kitchens of the old *gros bourg* families. Hyacinth Elwin's work has therefore also been a continuous learning experience as well as a crusade for improved nutrition on a national scale.

What we have here in this book is the result of years of note-taking and experimentation coupled with experience inherited, as she indicates in the dedication of this book, from her close family. It is the culmination of years of contact and exchange of ideas which reflects the very manner

vii

in which so much of Dominican culture has come about. The research in Part I enhances the experience of savouring the various dishes of Part II by being aware of the diverse origins of what we are eating.

The text is complemented by watercolour sketches from Loye Barnard and Sylvia Duckworth, which illustrate the traditional kitchens in which these recipes were once prepared. The old stone ovens and open range *potagé* cooking platforms are still to be seen around the island, although there are only a few still in use. The various utensils – graters, whisks, iron pots and 'lay lay' sticks – which formed the main *batterie de cuisine* for the cooks of centuries past are, however, still important kitchen equipment.

This taste of Nature Island cooking, therefore, is far more than a list of recipes: in sharing her extensive knowledge, Miss Elwin's deepens our understanding of this significant branch of Dominican heritage.

Lennox Honychurch

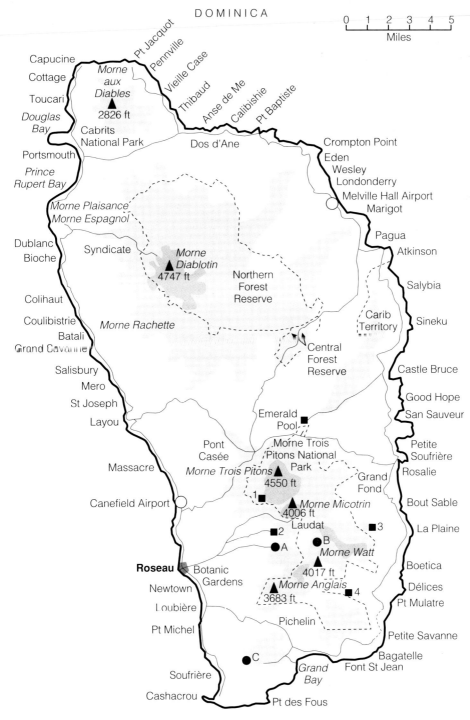

DOMINICA

0 1 2 3 4 5
Miles

Capucine
Cottage
Toucari
Douglas Bay

Pt Jacquot
Pennville
Vieille Case
Thibaud
Anse de Me
Calibishie
Pt Baptiste

Morne aux Diables
▲ 2826 ft

Cabrits National Park

Dos d'Ane

Crompton Point
Eden
Wesley
Londonderry
Melville Hall Airport
Marigot

Portsmouth
Prince Rupert Bay

Morne Plaisance
Morne Espagnol

Dublanc
Bioche

Syndicate

Morne Diablotin
▲ 4747 ft

Northern Forest Reserve

Pagua
Atkinson

Salybia

Colihaut
Coulibistrie
Batali
Grand Cavanne

Morne Rachette

Carib Territory

Sineku

Central Forest Reserve

Castle Bruce

Salisbury
Mero
St Joseph
Layou

Emerald Pool ■

Good Hope
San Sauveur

Pont Casée

Morne Trois Pitons National Park

Petite Soufrière
Rosalie

Massacre

Morne Trois Pitons ▲ 4550 ft

Grand Fond

Bout Sable

Canefield Airport ○

1 ■

▲ *Morne Micotrin* 4006 ft
Laudat

■ 3

La Plaine

Roseau ■ Botanic Gardens
Newtown
Loubière
Pt Michel

■ 2
● A

● B
Morne Watt ▲ 4017 ft

Morne Anglais ▲ 3683 ft

4 ■

Délices
Pt Mulatre

Pichelin

Petite Savanne

● C

Soufrière
Cashacrou

Grand Bay

Font St Jean
Bagatelle

Pt des Fous

■ FALLS: 1 Middleham Falls 2 Trafalgar Falls 3 Sari-Sari Falls 4 Victoria Falls
● SULPHUR SPRINGS: A Wotten Waven B Valley of Desolation C Grand Soufrière

Acknowledgements

This book grew out of a research project undertaken as part-fulfilment for the Diploma in Advanced Youthwork conducted by the Commonwealth Youth Programme: Regional Youth Development Centre, Guyana.

I am particularly indebted to all my friends and relatives who have encouraged me throughout. To the members of my household who seemed to have enjoyed the role of 'guinea pig' and were willing to 'taste', I shall always be grateful.

Special mention must be made of Mrs Dalia Carmel and Dr Jacqueline Newman whose encouragement finally made me resolve to put the study into book-form.

Many thanks go to Dame Mary Eugenia Charles for affording me the opportunity to realise my dreams.

Finally, deep appreciation is extended to Professor T H Henderson, my editor, for his invaluable advice, encouragement and willingness at all times to listen and discuss my ideas in a most professional manner.

Part I

The Dominicans and their culinary tradition

1

Historical background

On Sunday 3 November, 1493, Columbus and his followers made the first landfall, after leaving the Canaries. They were making their second voyage to the New World. Almost simultaneously four islands hoved into sight. The loftiest Columbus called Dominica, in honour of the day.

Dominica lies between the French departments of Martinique and Guadeloupe. It measures 29 miles long and 16 miles wide covering 290 square miles and has a population of 85 000. This island is the home of the last remaining Carib 'Indians' in the Caribbean Archipelago. Their population is 3500 and they live mainly on the north-east coast of the island.

Although the Caribs were dominantly a sea-faring people, they practised some agriculture. The main crops grown were cassava (*manioc*), sweet potatoes, corn, yams, beans, peppers, pumpkins and tannias. Cotton was grown for caulking canoes, household uses and, more particularly, for spinning into thread. The ochroe or annatto (*roucou*) was also grown and the red pulp covering the seeds used as 'war-paint' dye to smear on warriors before battle. It was also sometimes used as a source of food colouring, a practice observed in some villages, even today. The island possessed little wildlife (save manicou, agouti and birds), hence the diet of the Caribs consisted mainly of fish, root crops and maize. The island changed hands several times between European colonisers, mainly the British and the French, until 1802 when the British gained final possession.

European settlers were concerned mainly with producing goods for export to the North Atlantic seaboard, and consequently did not encourage the production of food for local consumption. Estate owners in the British Caribbean depended almost exclusively upon the continental American colonies for the supply of foodstuffs, livestock, and lumber with which to carry on building operations and construct containers for their produce. Grain cultivation and meat production were unprofitable enterprises for them.

Charcoal oven in estate 'great house'

The planter, for economic reasons, preferred to buy provisions from others rather than raise them by his own labour. The product of a single acre of his corn fields will purchase more Indian corn than can be raised in five times that extent of land, and pay besides the freight.[1]

The encroachment of the European races introduced to the Dominican gardens many food plants such as bananas, breadfruit, coffee, cocoa, dasheen, mangoes and plantain which were grown mainly for export both to North Atlantic shores and to the neighbouring French islands. Most food items were imported and it is expected that the food habits and recipes of the European continent were imported into Dominica by these settlers. The use in various forms of wheat flour, white potatoes, meat (beef, mutton), rice, saltfish (cod), pickled meat and milk are examples of early European introductions to the Dominican diet.

The British West Indies were developed as exploitation colonies ... Climatic conditions made an economic system based on free European workers impossible. Hence arose a regime of forced labour, resting first on the native Indian and, following virtual extinction, upon the more sturdy imported transatlantic black. This could be said to be the origin of negro slaves. The reason then was not moral, but for production.[2]

The African slaves were required to cultivate the sugar cane, coffee, indigo and other European-owned plantations on the island. The plantation owners provided the slaves with most of their food which consisted mainly of salted and pickled meats or fish, and flour imported from Europe. In addition, however, the slaves were allotted small garden plots on which they grew crops to supplement their diet. These crops included yams, tannias, dasheen, and coconut with which the Africans were familiar.

The life history of the individual is first and foremost an accommodation to the patterns and standards traditionally handed down in his community.[3]

Similarly the diet of the Dominican and the manner of preparation today bear evidence of the influence of the Caribs, French, English and Africans. Furthermore, acculturation through the mass media and greater contact with the wider world within the present century have influenced the dietary pattern and manner of food preparation of Dominicans, to the extent that there is a danger that the younger generation may not be exposed to the art of Dominican cooking.

However, since the attainment of independence in 1978, there has been a consciousness-raising of things Dominican and a thrust towards the preservation of one's own culture.

Living in small countryside communities, whether isolated or rural, has always required a certain amount of adaptability and resourcefulness. Recent years have seen many such communities looking back to the past for answers to today's ever-increasing costs, especially in the area of basic necessities.[4]

This has to a large extent been the Dominican experience. The coming of independence has brought in its wake the need to fall back on and develop every facet of one's natural resources and cultural experiences. With it has come the increased use of traditional dishes in the primary method of preparation, as well as innovations in preparing and presenting locally-grown foods. Increased knowledge, better education, more opportunities and facilities for learning have contributed in the main to the awakened interest in the Dominican cuisine particularly among the younger generation.

NOTES

1   Ragatz, Lowell J., *The Fall of the Planter Class in the British Caribbean, 1763 1883*, Octagon Books, New York, 1928
2   Taylor, Douglas, *Aspects of Dominican History*, Government of Dominica, Government Printing, 1967
3   Benedict, Ruth, *Patterns of Culture*, New American Library, Houghton Mifflin, 1993
4   Trovesicle, Lake, *The Rural Native Heritage Cookbook; The Gathering* Vol. 1, Native Women's Association.

2

Socioeconomic
and historical influences

Three groups of factors appear to mould eating patterns – the economic, the cultural and the historical factors. For economic, geographical or cultural reasons, diets in tropical countries tend to be based on a limited number of foodstuffs. The main bulk of the diet is usually composed of one or more carbohydrate staple eaten very often with smaller quantities of mixtures of various vegetables, relishes or sauces. The foregoing basically describes the Dominican diet.

The diet tends to consist mainly of the staple foods which are generally root crops such as dasheen, tannias, yams, cassava, and potatoes as well as other starchy foods such as green bananas, plantain and breadfruit.

The sociologist Kardiner theorises that the aspect of culture in which values find expression are in '... secondary institutions such as art, folklore, mythology and religion'.[1] The same argument can be applied to the use of food as a secondary institution, '... for food habits are the ways people have learned to select and consume foods',[2] taking into account such influences as their history and society.

Sociologists have observed that the vast proportion of all individuals who are born into any society always assume its behaviour, customs and beliefs which are not inherent but are learned through observation and instructions from parents and others. This is the significance of diffusion and its importance to food culture, for this is the main method by which the recipes have been learnt from the older folk or – to put it another way – using the traditional manner of passing on knowledge from grandmother to mother down to daughter. Our history has therefore tended to depend on oral rather than written accounts and unfortunately, as a result, much of its authenticity and richness has been either forgotten or lost.

Douglas Taylor, the anthropologist, says:

It is difficult at the present time to distinguish between these customs which belong to the Creole people in general, and those which are of genuine Carib origin.[3]

However, more of the Caribs' old customs than is believed have remained and are still practised.

Previous studies by Breton, Rouse and Taylor show that crabs and cassava were considered to be two of the Carib staple foods. It is also an established fact that the Caribs were renowned for fishing and hunting the wildlife which consisted mainly of possum (*manicou*) and agouti. They cultivated such crops as corn (maize), sweet potatoes, yams and peppers. It was their custom to use annatto (*roucou*) as war-paint as well as for cooking; and they cooked over the open fire. They also used the water of the cassava to produce a food preservative or sauce (cassareep). These practices are still used among the Caribs.

Fishing, hunting for wildlife, cooking on the open fire and the cultivation of similar crops are also practised by the Creoles. In that Taylor was correct but on closer examination, as will be seen from the recipes, the preparation differs. Thus the distinctive differences of food preparation by the two ethnic groups have survived other social changes which have taken place. What is most significant is that the Dominican cuisine has been influenced by four main cultures: Carib, French, British and African.

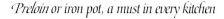

Preloin or iron pot, a must in every kitchen

Sylvia

Traditional preparation of foods brought by the British and French settlers have been adapted to the local foods and have been blended into a fascinating and varied cuisine. Present-day cooking still bears evidence of the French culture in the use of a particular type of pot used (the *cocote* or iron pot), the love of garlic and highly-seasoned foods. A typical Sunday dinner with the main dish of chicken which is enjoyed by Dominicans can also be traced to the French influence.

> 'I want there to be no more peasant in my kingdom to be so poor that he cannot have a chicken in his pot every Sunday,' declared Henry IV.[4]

Bouquet garni

The wide use of the *bouquet garni*, used especially by the older people, (tying together fresh parsley, a sprig of fresh thyme and a bay leaf), or the fine-herbs seasoning (which is a mixture of equal quantities of chopped fresh herbs) frequently used in seasoning meats and fish, are both derived from the French.

History has shown that the African slaves who were brought to the Caribbean proved very innovative and adaptable once they acquired stability (roots). They applied those qualities to their daily life and were able to maintain some practices and customs which came out of their culture. One area was growing the foods to which they were accustomed and maintaining their cooking and eating practices. Because of this the Dominican cuisine has been enriched.

The term 'provisions' used by the slaves to describe the root crops such as sweet potatoes, yams, dasheen and tannias is still used today by all Dominicans. These root crops comprised their staple foods and still provide the single largest amount of dietary energy, chiefly through their carbohydrate content.

However, to the credit of the slaves, their method of food preparation provided a balanced meal because of the use and addition of green leaves and vegetables to the one-pot which retained the nutritive value of the foods. As Dr Jelliffe put it:

> … most communities have by age-long experiment come to use foods in mixtures, so that their nutrients complement one another.[5]

The 'one-pot' or *braf* has remained one of Dominica's traditions in the culinary arts, and a good cook is often judged by his or her ability to cook a delectable braf. Wastage which may have occurred through loss of water, especially that of soluble vitamins, is retained in the water in which it is cooked and which is drunk. Heightened interest in better nutrition and healthy eating patterns has to a large extent attached great importance to the common one-pot method of cooking.

Ma Bello prepares her Sunday soup

Another practice, which is traced to our African heritage, is the serving of soup as the midday meal on a Sunday. Interestingly enough, this practice is more common in villages which have grown out of settlements in close proximity to one of the larger estates scattered around the country. In such a village there would be a police station, village school, post office, registrar of births and deaths and – most importantly – a church or several churches serving congregations within a radius of up to ten miles. It became the practice to prepare either a beef or tripe soup to serve visitors from outlying hamlets who visited family and friends after Mass. Supper, however, would consist of the traditional fowl (chicken) reared in the backyard, 'peas' (usually red kidney beans), rice or 'farine', (the parched hash of the cassava) and, of course, some root crops. This was followed by a cup of 'bush tea' (lime or orange leaves, for example, to aid digestion, or soursop leaves for a restful sleep).

Black pudding, a spicy, blood sausage, is another delicacy which originates from our African ancestry. It is served at parties, sold at fairs, food sales, in the shops and markets and it can truthfully be said that it transcends all social barriers.

The more sophisticated modes of food preparation which are mainly reserved for special occasions can be traced to the British influence. The tea party is the most practised. Although the practice of having afternoon tea is not observed as regularly as before, there are those who still invite friends and guests to tea at their homes. But the tea party as a fundraiser is very popular and is guaranteed to attract a crowd. The love of custard, tarts, pies, roast beef, candies and formal dinners can all be attributed to the British influence.

NOTES

1   Cajanus: Vol. 2 No. 4, 1973, Caribbean Food and Nutrition Institute, University of the West Indies, PO Box 40, Kingston 7, Jamaica
2   Leonard, Peter, *Sociology in Social Work*, Routledge & Kegan Paul, 1966
3   Taylor, Douglas, *Aspects of Dominican History*, Government of Dominica, Government Printing, 1967
4   Francy, Pierre, *New York Times – Sixty Minute Gourmet*, Fawcett Random House, Columbine, New York, 1979
5   Jelliffe, D.B., Cajanus: Vol. 6 No. 2, April–June 1973, Caribbean Food and Nutrition Institute, University of the West Indies, PO Box 40, Kingston 7, Jamaica

3

Ceremonies, festivals
and their associated foods

There are many traditional events and celebrations that remain important in the lives of Dominicans in spite of modernisation, acculturation and exposure to other influences. These events can be categorised into religious, national and secular. At some of the ceremonies the foods served may differ, depending on the occasion, but there are some foods that are served at all occasions and considered a 'must' as part of the Dominican cuisine.

Religious festivities

Dominicans love a *fête* and embrace every occasion for merry-making. They are a very out-going people and place great store on times set aside for jollification, festivity and socialising. By far the most celebrated religious festivals are Christmas and Easter followed by the village feasts associated with the patron saint of the particular village.

The preparation and celebrations which take place at Christmas are not very different from those in other Christian countries with the preceding excitement of shopping, the sound of Christmas carols on the radio interjected by the constant reminder of how many more shopping days left before Christmas. But the grand finale is the midnight Mass at the Roman Catholic churches with the singing of 'Cantique de Noel' at the stroke of midnight. This heralds in Christmas Day – a day mainly observed for a family gathering accompanied by the exchange of gifts, eating and drinking.

The eating and drinking begin immediately after Mass, when friends congregate at each others' homes to eat a braf made of smoked pork, a variety of yams (cush-cush, yellow yam, yam baba wolla), green bananas, dasheen, tannias, lots of hot pepper, lime, garlic, chives, onion and fresh thyme.

The smell of ham, turkey, pork, beef, black pudding (made from the blood and entrails of the pig), souse (made from the head and trotters of the pig), fachine (made from the cow's skin) all wafting in the breeze tell of the preparation for the Christmas Day fare. Not to be forgotten are the brewing of sorrel (a traditional drink made from the fleshy sepals of the rosella) and ginger beer; the baking of the Christmas cake (a dark fruit cake with lots of wine) and mastiff bread (hard dough bread); and the cooking of pigeon peas.

Christmas Eve in the rural areas is a busy day. The fattened pig is slaughtered very early that morning and the black pudding made; some of the pork and black pudding is sold and the remainder kept for family use. It is therefore not an unusual sight to see a temporary meat stall erected in a yard. Some of the tripe is left for soup the following day while the larger intestines are stuffed and salted and made into sausage (zandouge). This is strung up to be smoked over an open fire known as the *potagé* and used as flavouring in soups, vegetables, peas, or the inevitable *braf*.

A farm cottage

Feast days are associated with a patron saint. Many of the villages that do celebrate such days are fishing villages. The day usually begins with a church service to which fish is brought as an offering of thanksgiving. The service is then followed by a procession through the village accompanied by a rustic musical band. Socialising takes the form of both villagers and visitors going from house to house feasting and drinking. The revelry can go on well into the night.

Food and eating practices are inexplicably related to the practices, customs and behaviour of a community, regardless of whether it is a village or an urbanised sophisticated community. Serving *Chaudo* (eggnog) as the first drink to a child who has made his or her first communion is a practice still maintained throughout the country. So too is the practice of eating codfish or fresh fish in preference to a meat dish on Good Friday. Both of these practices are observed by followers of the Roman Catholic church *and* Protestant churches, which therefore characterises them more as cultural than religious.

National and secular festivals

Of great importance since attaining independence is the observance of Independence Day on 3 November. With it has come an awakening, revitalising, and a better understanding and appreciation of our cultural heritage.

The Friday before Independence Day is observed as Creole Day. At hotels, restaurants and at home Creole food is prepared and served. The Caribs maintain their traditional cooking; indeed it has been found that they have been less prone to innovation. One of their special dishes, pomkia, is a very old Carib recipe used on occasions when visitors are entertained.

While it is true that the observance of New Year's Day is not celebrated with the same verve as Christmas, nevertheless certain foods hold significance for the New Year. It is the practice to share the first meal of black-eye peas and rice cooked together with smoked pork. This meal is eaten after the Watch-night service and is supposed to bring good luck and prosperity.

Preparing for a picnic is great fun; but nothing compared with the excitement of cooking outdoors on the bank of a river over a fireplace hastily made up of three large stones capable of balancing the pot. The fire is fed by twigs and branches, easily found on the river bank, or with dried shells of coconuts.

The choice of food prepared and eaten would depend on the group at the picnic. Among a group of friends it would be normal to find the preparation of goat water (a light stew made from goat meat); souse (prepared from the pig's trotters or head); pelau (made with chicken); rice and peas (very highly seasoned). The more adventurous ones may be seen diving for fresh fish to be roasted in the fire and eaten with roasted breadfruit or plantains.

The less sophisticated but fun-loving picnickers might dam the river to form a small pool in which bottles of home-made ginger beer, rum, rum punch, passion-fruit drink and beers would be placed as a makeshift cooling device.

By contrast, at a family picnic all the food would be brought already prepared. Preference would therefore be given to those foods that transport easily such as macaroni and cheese, potato pie, baked or fried chicken, pelau, souse and black pudding. No picnic is worth its salt without rum punch and ginger beer, passion-fruit drink and beers.

Weddings, christenings, first communion or confirmation parties have been greatly influenced by modernisation and the effects of acculturation. This is not surprising since change takes place in human societies all the time. Sometimes it is so gradual that it is hardly perceptible to the extent that the members of the society themselves scarcely notice. Up to the early sixties it was customary to serve sanguire, a drink similar to a hot toddy made of unsweetened claret wine, spice, nutmeg and sugar as the first drink at a wedding. This has been replaced by a milk cocktail or – even more recently – by a coconut cocktail made from the milk of the dry coconut as the basic ingredient.

A wedding in the rural areas is a time of great festivity, with the rich fruit cake occupying central position. In some areas the practice of 'dancing' the cake is still practised. The cake is sometimes brought to the church and walked home to the wedding reception on the head or shoulder of a well-dressed woman. At the reception the dancing takes place. Partners are expected to dance around the cake and offer monetary donations. One of the reasons given for this ceremony is a means of helping to defray the expense of the cake which, if made in the correct proportions, can be costly.

A wedding is often a family occasion with members gathering from near and far to assist in the preparation of the food. Curried chicken, goat water and ground provisions such as yams, plantains, vegetable salad and rice are served in addition to savouries. As well as the wedding or bridal cake, there may be one or two other cakes – one of which is the groom's. But the cake everyone looks forward to tasting is the bridal cake which is served with wine at the high-point of the feasting.

In urban areas the influence of acculturation is most easily seen. While it was never the practice to 'dance' the cake, it used to be served with wine and was also the high-point of the feasting, but the practice now is to box the cake which is distributed thus to the guests. This has

Dancing the wedding cake

also lessened the use of, if not ruled out, the serving of wine, but champagne is served to toast the bride and groom during the usually lengthy round of speeches.

Again, the fare depends on the time of day of the wedding. While the practice of afternoon weddings continues to be observed, of recent times there have been early morning weddings followed by a breakfast, or mid-morning ceremonies with a luncheon after the ceremony. Appropriate foods are served making use of such local foods as codfish balls, titiri accra, souse, black pudding, crab backs, chicken and fish along with foods from international cuisines.

4

Types of cooking utensils and methods of food preparation

The types of pots and utensils people use vary depending on whether they live in an urban or rural area. This difference, though, has become less apparent with the advent of modern technology.

In the early days village homes would have a fire burning all day sometimes burning down to just embers and ashes which the housewife on her return from the field in the evening could easily rake up to prepare the main meal for the day.

The methods of heat used prior to the gas or electric stove were mainly three types. Kitchens were built separately and away from the dwelling house. The first type could be a simple covered shed to house a built up area to accommodate three stones on which the pot would rest. The fire would be ignited by lighting twigs and dried wood. A good draught would enable the wood to burn furiously at first and then to die down to a gentle heat. Those who could afford to would build the second type: a wooden kitchen with a *potagé* or open hearth constructed from red bricks cemented together to form two or three square holes with iron rods. The hearth would either be fired by charcoals or small twigs or the shell of dried coconuts. The more ingenuous would build a small oven at the bottom.

The third method would be the coalpot. This would be either locally made from clay or imported and made of cast iron. Coalpots are fired by charcoals.

However, because Dominica always has its share of hurricanes and heavy rainfall, it used to be customary for every household to own a small one or two burner kerosene stove which, in addition to being a stand-by in the event of an emergency, was often used to prepare the early morning coffee or tea.

Potagé (raised fireplace) with *galta*
for smoking meat and fish

The kerosene stove has now been largely replaced by propane gas and electric stoves. There are those who claim that the best cooked, and consequently best tasting, one-pot (*braf*) is the one prepared on a coal fire because:

> ... while the fire is burning furiously the vegetable absorbs the water but which also evaporates, and by the time the fire dies down the pot is barely simmering in a delicious liquor compounded of oil and vegetables and (meat or fish) juices. The fire has dictated the speed of the operation, the vegetables are tender, unbroken and retain their taste.[1]

This form of cooking is still used by a large number of families.

In 1979 Hurricane David devastated Dominica, people were forced to revert to many of the old practices of cooking including the coalpot which now holds a very prominent place in the kitchen once again. Most housewives, whether in the urban or rural area, own a coalpot, no longer put aside for the occurence of a natural disaster but used regularly to help cut down on the cost of gas and electricity.

Mention has been made in passing of the oven which some people built beneath their fire hearth. Baking has always been a form of cooking used – whether it was done in the earth, like the Caribs do, or in an oven. Before the advent of the present-day stove with an oven, the dome oven built of bricks was to be found in every village and town. Some are still in use today. In the good old days it was not unusual for people who lived close by or who were considered regular customers of a particular bakery to take along 'dishes' to the oven for baking when the heat of the oven was less intense. The baker was a very important person in the community: to him was entrusted the important role of baking wedding cakes, birthday cakes and Christmas cakes.

An old bread oven

Dome ovens are fired by dried wood which, when consumed to ashes, is swept out with a damp broom to sweep away as many of the ashes as possible before putting in the bread to bake. This type of bakery is also to be found in other parts of the world.

The descendants of slaves had to be inventive. Indeed some of the simple technology which they invented has, over the years, been developed into modern-day technology: for example grilling, barbecuing, baking, roasting and the use of the Dutch-oven. Those who did not have an oven asked the local tinsmith to build them a tin oven . This was then placed on a coalpot over the fire. The heat would rise through a hole in the bottom of the oven. Another method also used, particularly when baking either a milk custard or macaroni and cheese, was to pour the contents in an enamel dish, which would then be placed into an enamel plate with water and put to bake in an iron pot over a coal fire. The pot was then covered with a tin-sheet on which were placed burning coals. Here we see the introduction, as it were, of a simplified Dutch-oven. Those who did not have the luxury of an oven, or access to the use of one, found a way of baking a cake by using the method just described. The author's first attempt at baking a cake was to place the pan in a pot of water and fire it both from below and above. This proved to be as effective as baking it in a modern oven – albeit more time-consuming.

The Caribs were not pasturalists, but hunters and fishermen, so they had of necessity to devise some means of preservation and adopted the practice of smoking and drying their fish and meat. This practice still exists throughout the country. Smoked meat is one of the delicacies pre-pared at Christmas and carnival seasons, in particular. It is not unusual to see a *galta* or wooden grill erected over the fire from which hang meat or fish being smoked.

A variety of pots, containers and utensils were used in the past. They were mainly made of unglazed and glazed clay as well as of tin. Unglazed clay pots were used for cooking over the wooden fire as they could resist the heat. In the more sophisticated kitchen there was always a clay pot for cooking *fungi* or *coucou* made from cornmeal, an adapta-tion of the West African *foo-foo* made by crushing cassava, yam or plan-tain. Many a little girl was first introduced to cooking by being given her own clay pot to learn to cook like her mother or grandmother. Large glazed clay jars were reserved for salting meat (some of which went on to be smoked). Smaller jars were used to brew sorrel and local drinks used at Christmas, or for brewing ginger beer – a local drink made from ginger root.

Large clay pot, used for storing water and other items

The iron pot, *preloin* or *cocote*, was used for pot roasts and stews and is still found among the modern cooking utensils such as the pressure cooker, skillets and stainless-steel pots.

There are, however, some things that have disappeared. In the past no respected household would have been without a coffee mill and coffee pot. The pot was made by a local tinsmith. It contained three sections, each section a strainer of a different grade from which the coffee slowly dripped to the pot below. This has been replaced by the percolator. Its demise has been due largely to the fall in coffee production together with the availability and increased use of instant coffee. In some villages,

Coffee pot, fore-runner of the electric percolator

Coffee grinder and roasted coffee beans

however, local coffee is still roasted, ground or pounded, and brewed through a coffee bag. There is no real substitute for the aroma and taste of locally-grown, brewed coffee.

NOTE

1   Gray, Patience, *Honey From a Weed: Fasting and Feasting in Tuscany, Catalonia, the Cyclades and Apulia*, Harper & Row, London, 1986

5

Current influences on food use and food preparation

There is a sociological fact that must be taken into account in any understanding of cultural integration.[1]

In recent years many influences have made inroads to the traditional manner of preparation of foods. One influence has been that:

> ... nutritionists and dietitians in the region are understandably very concerned about the nutritional patterns and eating habits of a large section of the Caribbean Community. They wish to see effected a functional change in nutritional practices.[2]

This concern has brought about a greater diffusion of non-traditional practices through education programmes, both within the school system and through adult education classes. As a result housewives, cooks, and food vendors are better able to select and prepare healthy, varied and tasty recipes, while not discarding their own culture. Ever conscious of the cost factor, the importance of using foods in mixtures that ensure their nutrients complement one another, resulting in a balanced diet, is none the less emphasised.

Tourism, television and travel have also been influential and add a new flavour and dimension to the Dominican cuisine. Traditional dishes have been experimented with and have been reintroduced in the hotels and restaurants as very appetising and attractively-served meals.

In an effort to satisfy the tourists who visit our shores, chefs have added their own inventions, bringing an added richness out of the diversity of their experience; thus we have evidence of acculturation derived from experience, knowledge and exposure which has enriched the Dominican cuisine.

As mentioned the television, travel and migration have each played their part in the cultural integration such that Indian, Italian and

American cooking are now 'cheek by jowl' with African, French and British cooking. Barbecuing is by far the most popular. Barbecue parties are held frequently and barbecue chicken is sold at restaurants, night spots, dances and fairs. This form of cooking has become so popular that grills are now being manufactured locally. About ten years ago the sale of barbecue chicken along the streets on Carnival days was introduced. It has proved so popular that the sale of souse, black pudding, fried chicken, bakes and accra is fast disappearing.

The *roti*, introduced from Trinidad, is also in great demand, while the introduction of pizza, now a very popular fast food, has been more recent.

Modernisation and technology have also played their part. The formerly common sight of a woman in *wob dwiette* (national dress) with a round bamboo basket with bottles of home-made mauby and ginger beer on her head, complete with a lele or swizzle stick and glass, calling out her wares for sale, or of a woman with a wooden tray with small glasses or attractive glass jars filled with Floating island, is no longer to be seen in the streets of Roseau. In its place is the sale of locally-made fruit drinks freshly made from local fruits, in addition to the mauby and ginger beer. These are sold at hotels, restaurants, shops and are used in homes in preference to bottled drinks.

Churning ice-cream in the old-fashioned ice-cream tub had its compensation in receiving the dasher for hard work. This joy too has almost disappeared. There were women whose livelihood depended on making home-made ice-cream for sale. This has been replaced by the introduction of the Ice Cream Van, the Ice Cream Parlour with such brands as Häagen Daas for example.

Acculturisation is not only evident in the preparation of foods or the adoption of new cultural practices at the expense of some traditional ones: it is also found in the type of utensils used with the introduction of the pressure cooker, teflon pot, electric skillet, blender and mixer. The use of the microwave is steadily gaining popularity.

Paradoxically, in the late 60s a group adhering to the Rastafarian ideology sprang up. They prepared their *Itals* (food) very simply without salt or meat but made great use of fresh herbs, peas, beans and green leafy vegetables. They too, in their way, have influenced food use and preparation, for what has occurred is an increase in the production of herbs and vegetables with a greater supply in the market – ideal for Dominican cooks who delight in using fresh herbs and leafy vegetables.

Churning ice-cream for the Sunday luncheon dessert

NOTES

1   Benedict, Ruth, *Patterns of Culture*, New American Library, Houghton Mifflin, 1993
2   Henderson, T.H., 'Communication', Cajanus: Vol. 6, No. 3, July–September 1973, Caribbean Food and Nutrition Institute, University of the West Indies, P O Box 40, Kingston 7, Jamaica

6

Modern day influences

Although the pace of life in Dominica is still relatively easygoing the influences of the faster-paced communities can be seen in the country's eating habits, with the presence of Kentucky fried chicken, fish and chips, pizza and a number of other fast food outlets.

There are, however, local quick meals suited to the busy working mother with little time in which to prepare the midday meal, known as lunch, which still holds an important place in the Dominican diet. These local quick meals are generally healthier than the usually oil-based fast foods mentioned above.

The following are suggested quick meals which can be prepared well in advance with no fear of losing any of the food value.

Menu 1   Banana toad-in-the hole
Yellow split peas
Plain boiled rice
Tossed green salad
Soursop drink

Menu 2   Breadfruit cheese
Baked chicken
Coleslaw
Passion-fruit juice

Menu 3   Breadfruit pie
Steamed fish
Avocado pear slices
Tamarind drink

Menu 4   Yam pie
Curried beef stew
Christophine salad
Cherry juice

Menu 5   Banana salad
Fish pie
Steamed vegetable salad (carrots, christophine) with french dressing
Guava juice

Menu 6   Peas and rice
Codfish pie
Tomato, cucumber and lettuce (salad)
Lemonade

Menu 7   Banana meat loaf
Stewed red kidney beans
Tomato and lettuce salad
Passion-fruit juice

Part II

Dominican recipes

The following is a representative compilation of traditional Dominican recipes. For ease of reference, these have been placed into twelve 'family' groups under separate chapters.

NOTES:

1 Where quantities are measured in cups, one cup is equivalent to 8 oz (sugar).
2 Oven temperatures:

Oven heat	°C	°F	Gas no	Food type
cool	140 °C	275 °F	1	custards, egg dishes, milk puddings
slow	150 °C	300 °F	2	stews, rich fruit cakes
moderately slow	170 °C	325 °F	3	slow roasting, plain fruit cakes
moderate	180 °C	350 °F	4	sponge cakes, biscuits
moderately hot	190 °C	375 °F	5	small cakes
hot	200 °C	400 °F	6	shortcrust pastry, tarts
very hot	220 °C	425 °F	7	quick roasting, scones, bread
very hot	230 °C	450 °F	8	buns, rolls

Wooden mortar and pestle, indispensable tools in the old-time kitchen

1

Savouries and frying

Crab backs

6 crabs
2 cups soaked and minced bread
$\frac{1}{4}$ cup oil
1 clove garlic (crushed)
1 tablespoon ketchup
1 hot pepper (chopped)
$\frac{1}{2}$ cup chopped onion

2 tablespoons parsley (chopped)
breadcrumbs

Method
Wash and scald crabs in salt water. Put clean backs aside. Pick flesh off crab, secure fat – leave flesh on upper portion of six claws. Mix all ingredients except onions, parsley and breadcrumbs.

Put fat to heat; sauté onions, add mixture and keep stirring until mixture holds together (cook for about 15 minutes). Fill shells. Sprinkle with breadcrumbs.

Bake in a hot oven for 5–10 minutes. Decorate with parsley.

Clay dish used to marinate meat or fish

Sylvia

Black pudding

1 pint blood (pig or cattle)
$\frac{1}{2}$ lb entrails
5 bundles chives (chopped)
2 teaspoons minced hot pepper
10 local loaves (soaked overnight and
   minced)
$\frac{1}{2}$ lb pork fat (chopped)
  or $\frac{1}{4}$ pint corn oil
$\frac{1}{2}$ pint water
salt, to taste
juice of 1 lime

Method
Wash entrails thoroughly with lime
and test for holes. Tie length of
entrails at one end, set aside.

   Stew all ingredients (except blood
and water) in hot oil or fat. Remove
from fire, allow to cool slightly; then
add blood and water. Mixture must
be of pouring consistency.

   Fill entrails with mixture ensuring
that they are filled properly to get a
firmer pudding. Tie entrails at required
length for serving. Place in hot salt
water which is just below boiling
point. Do not allow water to boil. To
test for cooking prick with a pin: if oil
flows out the pudding is cooked.

Fachine

prepared cattle skin (from butcher)
juice of 1 lime
Brine:
$\frac{1}{2}$ hot pepper
juice of 1 lime
salt, to taste
2 blades chive (chopped)
1 clove garlic (crushed)
oil, to taste

Method
Procure prepared cattle skin from the
butcher. Boil skin in plain water until
soft. Remove from hot water and
submerge in cold water overnight.

   Prepare a brine of water –
sufficient to cover meat – chopped
chive, lime juice, hot pepper, garlic,
oil and salt to taste. Wash and clean
fachine in lime water. Cut into serving
pieces. Put in brine and leave for
1 hour before serving.

Souse

pig head or trotters
Brine:
pepper, lime, garlic, chive, thyme, salt

Method
Wash and cut up head or trotters. Put
to boil in salted water until soft. Cut
up in serving pieces. Make a brine (see
fachine above), and put meat in it to
stand. Can be left overnight.

   Serve with a cucumber salad.

Zandouge (smoked entrails) local sausage

entrails of pig
juice of 1 lime
8 green bay leaves
6 large hot peppers
cinnamon bark, approx 6″
1lb salt

Method
Wash and clean tripe (entrails) of pig thoroughly with lime juice. Pound together green bay leaves, hot peppers, cinnamon and salt. Place tripe in a container and cover with pounded mixture. Keep in this seasoning for 5–6 days.

Make a loop in a bit of string and into the loop fit as many of the small intestines as can be held.

Fill a large tripe with the small intestines on the loop. Tie the top tightly with a string, leaving a loop at the top to enable it to hang. Prick the bottom of the large, filled tripe for water to drain out.

Place over smoke until required.
Note: Pieces of zandouge can be used for flavouring in soups, mashed pawpaw, peas, boiled cucumber, etc.

Fresh seasoning herbs – every cook's delight

Frying

There are some foods which require frying including foods that are made in batter.

While shallow frying is the more popular form, deep fat frying is used for *accras* – fritters made from fish and local food staples. The very popular *titiri accra*, is made from the minute river fry called titiri.

Tannia and bean cakes

(Serves 6)
$\frac{1}{2}$lb black eye peas
1 lb soft white tannias
2 blades chive (chopped)
salt and pepper, to taste

oil, for frying

Method
Soak peas overnight in warm water. Next morning rub them between hands to remove skin. Pound pulp in a mortar.

Peel tannias and grate raw. Mix together with pounded peas, chive, and salt and pepper to taste.

Drop by spoonfuls into hot deep fat, fry till brown.

Titiri accra

2 cups titiri
2–3 blades chive (chopped)
salt, to taste
$\frac{1}{2}$teaspoon grated nutmeg
$\frac{1}{2}$hot pepper (chopped finely)
1 cup water
flour, as required

oil, for frying

Method
Soak and wash titiri thoroughly, being careful to remove straw and sand. Add chopped chive, pepper, salt, nutmeg and water. Using flour as required, mix to form a creamy paste.

Drop by spoonfuls into hot oil. Fry to a crisp golden colour.

Should be prepared $\frac{1}{2}$ hour before time to serve.

Yam puffs

(Serves 6)
1 lb yams
2 tablespoons butter
pinch of salt
4 eggs

oil, for frying

Method
Peel, wash and boil yams. Mash, while hot, with butter and salt. Add whole eggs. Mix together.

Drop by spoonfuls into deep fat. Fry to a crisp golden colour.

Codfish accra

(Makes 40)
$\frac{1}{4}$ lb codfish
1 cup flour
2 cups water
2 teaspoons baking powder
Seasoning:
1 hot pepper (chopped finely)
1 blade chive (chopped finely)
1 small onion (chopped finely)
1 sprig parsley (chopped finely)
2 teaspoons curry power (optional)

oil, for frying

Method
Boil and mince codfish together with seasoning. Add flour and baking powder. Mix together. Add water, stirring constantly; mixture should be of a dropping consistency.

Fry by spoonfuls in hot oil until a golden brown colour.

Breadfruit puffs

1 breadfruit
2 tablespoons butter
2 blades chive (chopped)
1 onion (chopped)
1 egg
salt, to taste
breadcrumbs

oil, for frying

Method
Boil breadfruit and mash while hot. Mix in butter, chive, salt and onion. Add egg, beat well.

Roll mixture into balls. Toss in breadcrumbs and fry in hot oil until a crisp, golden brown.

Sweet breadfruit accra

$\frac{1}{2}$ sweet or soft breadfruit
1 teaspoon sugar
pinch of salt
pinch of black pepper
2 tablespoons flour
1 blade chive (chopped)
1 small onion (chopped)
$\frac{1}{4}$ lb cooked minced codfish
2 tablespoons milk
1 teaspoon baking powder

oil, for frying

Method
Peel breadfruit and put in a mixing bowl. Add the remainder of the ingredients and beat together.

Drop by spoonfuls into boiling fat. Fry to a golden brown.

Beigner Creole-style

1 *cup flour*
1 *cup water*
$\frac{1}{4}$ *cup butter*
1 *whole vanilla bean or 1 tablespoon*
  vanilla essence
4 *eggs*

oil, for frying
icing sugar
powdered cinnamon

Method
Put water, butter, vanilla bean *or* vanilla essence in a pan. Bring to the boil. When boiling, pour in flour all at once. Keep stirring. Lower heat and cook until mixture forms into a ball and sides of the pan are clean. Leave mixture/roux to cool.

Add eggs, one at a time, until well mixed. (If using an electric mixer, use No 4 speed.)

Drop by spoonfuls into hot, but not boiling, oil. Remove when golden brown and puffed up.

Place on absorbent paper and sprinkle with 7 parts of sifted icing sugar to 1 part of powdered cinnamon.

Spinach-leaf accra

two dozen spinach leaves
1 *clove garlic (chopped)*
$\frac{1}{2}$ *onion (chopped)*
1 *teaspoon baking powder*
1 *cup flour*
$\frac{1}{2}$ *teaspoon curry powder*
pinch of black pepper
salt, to taste

oil, for frying

Method
Allow spinach leaves to boil for fifteen minutes. Remove from fire and chop.

Mix thoroughly with the remainder of the ingredients.

Fry by spoonfuls in hot oil. Serve hot.

2

Cereals

Corn porridge

1 lb fresh ground corn
2 cups milk (either cow's milk or
    coconut milk)
$\frac{1}{4}$ teaspoon nutmeg (grated)
1 cup water
$\frac{1}{2}$ cup sugar
1 small piece cinnamon

Method
Bring water, nutmeg and cinnamon to
the boil. Add milk and sugar. Allow
to reach boiling point. Lower heat
and pour in ground corn, stirring
constantly to prevent sticking.

Farine porridge

$\frac{1}{2}$ pint farine (see page 73)
1 cup coconut milk
$\frac{1}{2}$ cup water
$\frac{1}{2}$ teaspoon salt
1 teaspoon spice (cinnamon)
1 cup sugar

Method
Bring milk, water, salt and spice to
the boil. Gradually add farine, stirring
constantly to avoid lumps. Add sugar.
    If a thinner porridge is desired,
add more milk.

3

Soups

Soups should be cooked on a slow fire over an open fire, using a coalpot, or on a gas or electric stove burner. Slow cooking is considered the best method to ensure that proper consummation takes place, which is guaranteed to bring out the rich flavour of the ingredients.

The basic ingredients for Callalou soup are the young leaves of the tannia or dasheen, with ochroes. Spinach leaves and callalou leaves can also be used.

Seasonings such as thyme, chive, celery leaves, basil, and garlic are used as fresh herbs in soups, in preference to dried herbs.

Soups, with the addition of ground provisions (potatoes, tannias, eddoes, etc.) or breadfruit and dumplings (– and in some soups small chunks of meat – beef or pork), are served as a main meal.

For formal occasions soup is served as the first course (or entrée). As a first course the boiled mixture is whisked then strained, or liquidised in a blender. It is generally served without the tuber or dumplings but may be served with bread.

Crapaud (frog legs) soup

(Serves 4)
2 crapauds
juice of 1 lime
3–4 potatoes (diced)
4 carrots (diced)
1 small onion (sliced)
1 clove garlic (crushed)
1 oz macaroni
5 cloves
1 sprig leeks
1 turnip (diced)
1 sprig celery
2 tablespoons table butter
salt and pepper, to taste

Method
Clean and cut up crapaud. Squeeze lime juice over meat. Sprinkle with salt and pepper.

Put carrots and potatoes to boil in 2 pints of water. Add whole leek and celery and boil for 20 minutes. Add cloves, onions, crapaud, garlic and macaroni. Leave to simmer for another 20 minutes. Add butter, salt and pepper to taste.

If soup is to be served as a first course, strain and serve. If it is to be served as a main dish, serve with all vegetables.

Breadfruit soup

(Serves 4)
1 lb soup bones
1½ lb breadfruit (cut into 1" squares)
1 green pepper (chopped)
Seasoning:
1 small onion (chopped)
1 sprig celery (chopped)
salt, to taste

1 sprig parsley, for decoration

Method
Wash soup bones; put to boil in
3 pints of water for 1 hour. Wash and
add breadfruit to liquid. Boil until
breadfruit is tender.
　　Add seasoning, salt and pepper to
taste. Decorate with chopped parsley.

Callalou (1)

(Serves 4)
2 bundles young dasheen leaves
　　or chock Martinique (tannia leaves)
½ lb salt meat cut up into small bits
1 small onion (chopped)
1 coconut (grated)
Seasoning:
2 blades chive (chopped)
1 sprig thyme
1 clove garlic

Method
Chop leaves finely. Put to steam with
meat bits and onion. Do not add any
water. Stir occasionally to enable
leaves to melt. Season to taste.
　　Add milk extracted from grated
coconut (see Glossary, page 112) and
simmer for 10 minutes before serving
hot.

Callalou (2)

(Serves 7)
2 bundles dasheen leaves
8 ochroes
1 onion (chopped)
2 blades chive (chopped)
1 sprig celery
½ cup dry coconut (grated)
salt and pepper

Method
Wash and chop dasheen leaves. Cut
ochroes into small pieces and add
whole celery, chopped onion and chive.
　　Grate coconut and extract milk
(see Glossary, page 112). Add enough
water to make 2½ pints milk. Add
coconut milk to other ingredients.
Bring to the boil. Add salt and pepper
to taste. Boil until leaves and ochroes
are tender enough to press through
sieve (or strainer). Served strained
mixture hot.
　　Callalou can also be liquidised in
a blender.

Ingredients for a tasty callalou

Callalou (3)

4 *bundles young dasheen leaves*
1 *lb beef* or *mutton*
2 *turnips (chopped)*
2 *large carrots (chopped)*
salt and pepper
3 *tannias* or *potatoes (diced)*
vermicelli (optional)
Seasoning:
1 *onion (chopped)*
1 *clove garlic*
3 *cloves*

Method
Wash and chop leaves. Put together with meat to boil until soft. Add seasoning, carrot and turnips.

Peel, wash and dice tannias (or potatoes), add to pot with vermicelli (if desired). Add water as required; salt and pepper, to taste.

Callalou (4)

1 bundle dasheen leaves
4 oz pumpkin (diced)
1 lb smoked pork
4 oz pigeon peas
2–3 tannias
1 tablespoon margarine
2–3 tablespoons oil
1 packet chicken noodle soup
   (optional)
tomato ketchup
Lea & Perrins Sauce (optional)
salt, to taste
Seasoning:
2 small onions (chopped)
2 blades chives
1 sprig thyme
1 sprig parsley
1 sprig celery
2 cloves garlic
1 whole green pepper

$\frac{1}{2}$lb flour (for dumplings)

Method
Clean and chop leaves. Put to boil (with meat that has been soaked) in sufficient water to cover leaves. Add pumpkin and peas. When meat is tender add water according to quantity required.

Make flour dumplings (recipe on page 74) and add to pot together with chopped tannias. Add all other ingredients and simmer for 20 minutes.

Callalou (5)

1 bundle dasheen leaves
$\frac{1}{2}$lb pickled meat
6 ochroes
bouquet garni
1 clove garlic (crushed)
3 plantains ⎫
$\frac{1}{2}$lb tannias ⎬ ground provisions
$\frac{1}{2}$breadfruit ⎭
1 green pepper
2 tablespoons coconut cream
1 tablespoon butter
2 tablespoons oil

$\frac{1}{2}$lb flour (made into dumplings –
   see page 74)

Method
Clean and chop leaves. Cut ochroes into pieces.

Put meat to boil with sufficient water to cover. Add leaves and ochroes; boil until meat is tender and leaves have melted. Add ground provisions and bouquet garni and one whole green pepper. Boil for a further 20 minutes. Add dumplings, garlic, coconut cream, butter and oil and simmer for 15 minutes.

Spinach soup

1 bundle spinach
2 blades chive
1 medium onion (sliced)
salt and pepper
White sauce:
2 tablespoons margarine
$\frac{1}{2}$ cup flour
1 cup milk

Method
First make the white sauce. Melt the margarine over low heat. Then slowly add the flour, stirring all the time. Remove from heat and gradually add the milk and stir until the sauce thickens. Put to one side whilst preparing the spinach.

Remove leaves from stalks. Place in boiling water in uncovered pan. Add chive and onion. Boil for five minutes. Remove from fire. Pour cold water over the cooked leaves and strain.

To white sauce add the chopped, cooked leaves. If too thick dilute with milk or water to required consistency. Season to taste.

Breadnut soup

3 lb breadnuts
4 oz salt beef (cut into cubes)
1 lb pork (cut into cubes)
seasoning (of choice)
salt and pepper

Method
Boil breadnuts in salted water. Scoop from shells, cut in halves and remove brown skin covering nuts. Pound to a smooth paste and set aside.

Put beef and pork together in a pan in unsalted water with combined seasoning; bring to the boil.

Add pounded breadnuts to meats; boil, stirring occasionally until smooth.

Pumpkin soup (1)

(Serves 6)
$\frac{1}{2}$ small pumpkin
2 pints milk or coconut milk (see
   Glossary, page 112)
1 onion (chopped)
2 blades chive (chopped)
1 tablespoon butter
2 tablespoons vegetable oil
1 tablespoon lard
salt and pepper

Method
Peel and cube pumpkin, put to boil in 1 pint water. When cooked remove from the fire and mash finely. Add milk.

Place butter, oil and lard to heat in a saucepan. Add chopped onion and chive. Stew gently. Add to pumpkin mixture; stir and allow to simmer for 10 minutes. Add salt and pepper to taste.

Pumpkin soup (2)

2 lb pumpkin
$\frac{1}{2}$ lb tannias
bouquet garni
salt and pepper
2 tablespoons table butter
1 tin evaporated milk

Method
Peel and dice pumpkin and tannias.
Allow to boil in 2 pints water until
soft. Add bouquet garni. Remove
from fire. Mash (or swizzle).

Return to fire and simmer for
10 minutes. Add milk, salt and pepper
to taste, and butter while simmering.

Pumpkin soup (3)

1 lb salt beef or pig tail
$\frac{1}{2}$ lb tannias (chopped)
6 ochroes or 1 bundle spinach
   (chopped)
bouquet garni
1 clove garlic
2 tablespoons margarine
2 lb pumpkin (in chunks)
$\frac{1}{2}$ lb flour (for droppers)
pepper, to taste

Method
Put meat to boil with sufficient water
to cover. When meat is tender add
chopped pumpkin, tannias and
ochroes. Test water for saltiness. If
too salty remove some water and
replace with required amount of
water. Bring to the boil and boil until
pumpkin chunks are tender, remove
these, crush and return them to pot.

Make droppers (see 'flour
dumplings' on page 74) and add to
pot with all other ingredients. Simmer
for a further 10 minutes.

Young ochroes

Cow-heel soup

2 cow heels
juice of 1 lime
6 cups water
1 onion (chopped)
2 carrots (diced)
1 tablespoon barley
1 large tannia (diced)
$\frac{1}{2}$ teaspoon black pepper
bouquet garni
salt, to taste

Method
Wash cow heels in lime juice. Cut up and bring to the boil in salted water. Skim frequently. Cook for 2 to 3 hours over low heat.

Add vegetables, salt and pepper, bouquet garni and barley. Boil until vegetables are tender. It may be necessary to add more water. Serve hot.

Tripe soup

4 lb tripe
$\frac{1}{2}$ cup white vinegar
2 potatoes (diced)
2 cups diced carrots
1 oz vermicelli
1 oz table butter
salt and pepper
6 cups + 1 gallon water
2 teaspoons barley (optional)
Seasoning:
2 small onions (chopped)
1 sprig each of chive, thyme, parsley

Method
Soak tripe in vinegar with enough water to cover. Allow to soak for 2 hours, drain, and rinse with water.

In 1 gallon of water bring tripe to the boil, skim, then cook over low heat for 3 hours. Strain and cut tripe into small pieces, then set aside.

Place potatoes, carrots, vermicelli, barley and seasoning with six cups of water and bring to the boil. Allow to boil for about $\frac{1}{2}$ hour, then add pieces of tripe, butter, and salt and pepper to taste. Simmer for ten minutes until soup thickens in consistency.

4

Vegetables

Pawpaw au gratin (1)

1 medium-sized green pawpaw
1 onion (chopped)
1 clove garlic (crushed)
pinch black pepper
1 small tin evaporated milk
4 oz cheese (grated)
salt

oil, for stewing
breadcrumbs

Method

Peel, boil and mash pawpaw.

Place garlic and onion in hot oil, stir for $\frac{1}{2}$ minute. Pour mashed pawpaw together with pinch of black pepper into garlic and onion mixture. Allow to stew. Add milk, grated cheese and salt to taste. Leave mixture to stew for a few minutes longer.

Pour into greased dish. Sprinkle with breadcrumbs.

Either grill or bake in a medium oven until top is browned.

Pawpaw au gratin (2)

1 medium-sized green pawpaw
1 onion (chopped)
coconut milk
1 tablespoon flour
Seasoning:
chive, thyme, garlic
salt and pepper

oil, for frying
breadcrumbs

Method

Peel, boil and mash pawpaw.

Heat oil; pour in mashed pawpaw and onions. Stir. Add coconut milk gradually, stirring all the time. Add flour-paste (water and flour), seasoning, salt and pepper to taste. Allow to stew.

Pour into greased baking dish, sprinkle with breadcrumbs. Bake if desired.

43

Belongene (egg-plant) in batter

2 or 3 belongenes
vinegar
salt
white pepper
$\frac{1}{4}$cup flour
1 egg (beaten)
$\frac{1}{4}$cup water

oil, for frying

Method
Peel and slice belongene. Soak in water to which salt, vinegar and white pepper have been added.

While soaking is in progress, prepare a batter of flour, water, egg, salt and pepper, to taste.

Pat slices of belongene with a clean towel until dry. Dip each slice in batter and fry in hot oil until golden brown.

Belongene (egg-plant) Creole

(Serves 4)
3 large egg-plants
2 onions (chopped)
2 sweet peppers (sliced)
1 clove garlic (crushed)
2 tablespoons margarine
1 large tomato (sliced)
2 tablespoons tomato sauce
$\frac{1}{4}$cup water
salt and pepper, to taste

Method
Slice the egg-plant very thinly and boil in salt water until tender. Drain carefully and set aside.

Heat margarine and sauté onions, peppers, tomato and crushed garlic for 5 minutes. Add tomato sauce, water, salt and pepper. Allow to simmer for 3 minutes. Put in the egg-plants.

Remove from heat and pour into serving dish.

Callalou (Carib)

24–36 young dasheen leaves
1 teaspoon curry powder
$\frac{1}{2}$teaspoon black pepper
3 cloves
1 clove garlic
$\frac{1}{8}$pint oil
2 tablespoons vinegar
salt

Method
Peel off outer skin of leaf stalks, cut up the remaining leaves and boil in salt water. When cooked, mash. Add the remaining ingredients. Pour into a shallow dish, cover and shake gently. Leave to stand until ready for use.

Codfish, meat, fish or pig snout may be added to this preparation.

West Indian avocado (egg plant),
the gourmet's favourite

Green pawpaw

1 medium-sized green pawpaw
Seasoning:
1 teaspoon curry powder
$\frac{1}{2}$ teaspoon black pepper
3 cloves
1 clove garlic
$\frac{1}{8}$ pint oil
2 teaspoons vinegar
salt, to taste

Method
Peel pawpaw and put to boil. When
cooked, slice thinly. Spoon mixed
seasoning over pawpaw and set aside.
Use as a vegetable.

Seasoned pumpkin

1 lb pumpkin
$\frac{1}{2}$ onion (chopped)
1 blade chive (chopped)
$\frac{1}{2}$ sweet pepper (chopped)
1 tablespoon margarine
salt and pepper, to taste
juice of $\frac{1}{2}$ lime

breadcrumbs

Method
Peel pumpkin and put to boil in salt
water. When cooked, crush and
season with other ingredients (except
margarine). Beat in margarine.

Pour into a greased dish, sprinkle
with breadcrumbs. Bake in a hot oven
for 5 minutes.

Travels with a donkey

Stuffed christophine

(Serves 6)
6 christophines
2 egg yolks
$\frac{1}{4}$ cup milk
1 tablespoon flour
2 blades of chive (chopped)
salt and pepper, to taste

grated cheese for topping

Method
Peel christophines. Cut in half lengthwise and remove cores. Add salt to water and boil until tender.

For each christophine: cut about $\frac{1}{2}''$ from one end, put aside. Scoop out inside leaving $\frac{1}{2}''$ wall thickness (shells). Crush scooped-out portion.

Beat yolk of eggs, add milk, flour, chive, salt and pepper; mix well.

Stir mixture into crushed christophine.

Fill shells with mixture and top with grated cheese. Bake in oven (300 °F) for approximately $\frac{1}{2}$ hour, or until brown.

Christophine au gratin

3 large christophines
1 small onion (chopped)
1 clove garlic (crushed)
black pepper
2 tablespoons + 1 teaspoon oil
breadcrumbs

Method
Peel christophines and boil in salt water. Crush when cooked. Mix onion, garlic and a dash of black pepper into crushed christophines.

Heat two tablespoons oil in a pan and pour in mixture. Leave to stew on medium heat. Pour into a greased dish. Cover with breadcrumbs and sprinkle one teaspoon oil on top.

Place in moderate oven and cook until brown.

Crème de christophine

6 medium-sized christophines
2 oz margarine
2 oz lard
6 oz flour
$\frac{1}{2}$ pint milk
1 onion (sliced)
salt and pepper, to taste

Method
Peel and thinly slice christophines. Put to boil in unsalted water. When cooked, lay slices in a dish.

Make a thick white sauce with other ingredients including the onion. Pour over slices of christophine. Allow to cool before serving.

5

Fish and shellfish

Fish is prepared in a variety of ways depending on the occasion.

The most common method of cooking fish is the **coubouillon** method or plain boil, when the broth of the fish is thickened with a roux.

Salted codfish or pickled fish, such as mackerel, is popular. Often a white sauce or cheese sauce is prepared as accompaniment to the salted fish.

Pan frying is another popular method. Sometimes the fish is fried before it is boiled in a sauce known as a 'brown stew'.

Roasting, grilling, or barbecuing are also methods used. Choice of method depends largely on the type of fish and the occasion when it is served.

Roasting is often used to prepare smaller fish such as sprats, sardines, ballahoue and dried salted fish like flying fish, codfish and smoked herring.

Grilling is used for the larger and firmer-fleshed fish such as snapper, tuna and cavally.

Barbecuing fish has become very popular particularly for village fish fetes, parties or picnics. Barbecued fish can be obtained any weekend at roadside barbecue stands.

The practice of **smoking** fish, which has first been boned and salted, is still a custom in the rural areas, especially during that time of year when there is a glut of fish on the market. The thrifty housewife does not only preserve the fish for home consumption, but also uses it as a form of barter by taking some of it to the market and using the money earned to purchase other basic staples.

Fish

Fish coubouillon (plain boiled fish)

2 lb fish (red fish, tuna, dolphin, blue
  robin or jacks)
2 oz butter
$\frac{1}{8}$ pint cooking oil
2 blades chive (chopped)
1 clove garlic (crushed)
juice of 2 limes
1 tablespoon flour
1 hot pepper
salt and pepper

Method
Clean fish and put to soak in a
mixture of water, salt, hot pepper and
juice of 1 lime. Leave for two hours.

Heat pot at medium heat, then
add oil and butter; stir until butter is
melted; add chive and garlic. Cook
lightly, then add fish and 1 cup water.
Allow to boil. Add remaining lime
juice, salt and pepper to taste.
Thicken slightly with a mixture of
flour and water. Cover and simmer
for 5 minutes.

Serve hot.

A tasty fish stew requires a lot of fresh seasoning

Codfish bulljaw

1 lb codfish
2 onions (chopped)
1 sprig parsley
1 sprig celery (chopped)
$\frac{1}{2}$ sweet pepper (chopped)
1 hot pepper
1 clove garlic
1 tablespoon curry powder
1 teaspoon mustard
salt and pepper

oil, for stewing

Method
Soak codfish overnight in water.
Drain and bring to the boil three
times, each time draining and
replacing water. After boiling, remove
bones (if any), and grind to a mince
with onions, parsley, celery, sweet
pepper, hot pepper and garlic. Stir in
curry powder, mustard, salt and
pepper to taste. Stew mixture in hot
oil.
Serve as filling for local bread.

Codfish coubouillon (1)

(Serves 6)
1 lb codfish
1 large onion (sliced)
2 oz table butter
2 pints fresh cow's milk
1 teaspoon flour
black pepper and salt

Method
Wash codfish thoroughly, add water
and allow to boil for 15 minutes.
Drain and flake.
Fry onion lightly in melted
butter. Add cow's milk, flaked
codfish, black pepper and (if desired)
salt to taste. Mixture may be
thickened using flour. Leave to
simmer for 5 minutes before serving.

Codfish coubouillon (2)

1 lb codfish
1 large onion (sliced)
4 tablespoons oil
2 tablespoons lard
1 clove garlic
1 teaspoon flour
1 tablespoon vinegar
1 pint water

Method
Boil codfish to remove the salt. Clean
and flake.
Sauté onion in heated oil and
lard. Add water and flaked codfish;
allow to boil. Add vinegar and garlic,
thicken with flour if required. Simmer
for 5 minutes.
Serve with ripe plantains, yam
and pigeon peas.

Twin sisters off the Calibishie beach

Codfish au gratin

1 lb codfish
1 lb potatoes
1 large onion (chopped)
1 blade chive (chopped)
2 oz table butter or margarine
$\frac{1}{8}$ pint oil
1 small tin evaporated milk

breadcrumbs
parsley to garnish

Method
Soak codfish overnight.
　　Peel and boil potatoes. Clean and flake codfish. Grind to a mince together with potatoes.
　　Heat oil and butter in a saucepan. Sauté onions and chive. Add potatoes and codfish, mix well. Add milk gradually, beating mixture thoroughly to a creamy consistency. Pour into greased dish and smooth top of mixture with a little oil. Sprinkle with breadcrumbs. Mark into squares.
　　Bake in a moderate oven for about 15 minutes. Decorate with parsley.

Codfish sancoche

1 lb codfish
1 large onion (sliced)
1 clove garlic (crushed)
1 blade chive (chopped)
1 tablespoon oil
½ pint coconut milk (see Glossary,
    page 112)
1 teaspoon flour, if desired
black pepper, to taste

Method
Wash codfish thoroughly, remove
bones, add water and boil for
15 minutes; drain and flake.
    Fry onion, chive and garlic lightly
in oil. Add coconut milk, flaked
codfish, black pepper and simmer for
5 minutes. Thicken with flour if
desired.
    Serve with hard boiled eggs.

*Dominica limes, essential in fish dishes and a
must for a fortifying rum punch*

Roast fish (Red fish or carangue)

fish (quantity of choice)
2–3 medium onions (cut into rings)
1 clove garlic (crushed)
oil, vinegar, salt

1 large lime ⎫
parsley   ⎬ to garnish
                ⎭

Method
Clean fish and cook over open fire.
Place in a dish and cover with onion.
    Make a vinaigrette sauce using
garlic, salt, oil and vinegar. Beat well
until it thickens. Pour mixture over
fish.
    Decorate with parsley and slices
of lime.

Ton pitché (stuffed tuna)

2 lb round of ton (tuna), 2" thick
Stuffing:
1 large onion
2 cloves garlic (crushed)
1 blade chive
$\frac{1}{4}$ lb salted pork fat or 2 rashers of
    bacon
$\frac{1}{2}$ hot pepper

Method 1:
1 sprig thyme
2 blades chives
1 onion
2 cloves garlic
1 tablespoon butter
$\frac{1}{2}$ cup oil
juice of 1 lime
salt and pepper

flour, as required

Method 2:
1 sprig celery
oil, as required
flour, as required

Preparation
Scale and thoroughly clean fish. Put to soak overnight in brine (see page 30).

The following day chop 1 onion, 2 cloves garlic, 1 blade chive, bacon (if used), $\frac{1}{2}$ pepper and mix together.

Remove fish from brine. Wipe with a clean cloth and, using the point of a sharp knife, scoop holes about $\frac{1}{2}$" deep in flesh of fish. Fill holes with chopped mixture. Cover the holes with the flesh removed.

Method
Now that the tuna is ready it can be cooked in one of two ways.
1 *Either:*
Make a bouquet garni with the thyme and chives. Put the heated oil and butter in a hot iron pot together with the onion (sliced) and garlic; sauté lightly. Add prepared fish; cover and leave to stew for 15 minutes, turning fish at intervals. Pour in sufficient water to make a gravy adding lime juice, salt and pepper to taste.

Thicken the gravy slightly with flour and simmer for a further 15 minutes.
2 *or:*
Coat fish with flour and fry in deep fat. Decorate with chopped celery. Serve with brown gravy.

Fish sancoche

(Serves 6)
1 lb tuna (or any other fish)
1 coconut (grated)
2 cloves garlic (crushed),
1 small onion (chopped),
2 blades chive (chopped)
1 teaspoon ochroe
1 teaspoon flour
salt and pepper, to taste

butter ⎫
⎬ *for stewing*
oil ⎭

Method
Clean fish and cut in serving pieces. Season with salt and pepper, and fry.

Make a gravy by adding water to grated coconut and squeezing juice out until the required amount of gravy is made.

To heated pot add butter, oil, chopped chive, garlic and onion. Allow to stew. Add juice of coconut (gravy) and ochroe, then bring mixture to the boil; make a paste with flour and water and stir into the mixture to thicken. Allow to boil; add fish, salt and pepper to taste. Simmer for 5 minutes.

Smoked fish

Smoked herring bulljaw

1 lb smoked herring
1 teaspoon mustard
dash Lea & Perrins sauce
2 tablespoons tomato sauce

Seasoning:
2 onions (chopped)
1 sprig parsley
½ sweet pepper (chopped)
1 hot pepper
1 clove garlic (crushed)

Method
Boil smoked herring until cooked. Drain and remove bones. Mince together with all seasoning. Add mixture of mustard, Lea & Perrins sauce and tomato sauce; stir well. Stew in hot oil.

Serve in bread or in bouchée cases.

Smoked fish

3 lb dolphin or *flying fish*
$\frac{1}{4}$*lb rock salt (pounded)*

The traditional way of smoking fish is to first prepare a *boucan*.

The preparation of a boucan
At an open fireplace, or firepit, a fire is lit. Logs are then placed on the fire and covered with dry ground provision peelings, green banana peel, or dry coconut husks. This will create the smoke.

A stand is made above the fire with four upright sticks and cross sections of smaller, thinner rods – about 2″ apart, on which prepared fish is placed for smoking.

Method
Clean fish properly. Gash fish in order to open sides. Rub pounded salt into gashes. Place in a container and leave overnight.

The prepared fish is then placed on the *boucan* with the salted section towards the fire, and covered with green banana leaves. Allow to smoke for about 3 days.

When the process is complete, the fish should be golden brown. Fish smoked in this manner will last for months.

To cook
Put fish in boiling water. When cooked, flake.

Serve with either a white sauce or brown gravy. Decorate with slices of hot pepper.

Shellfish

Daub crab

(Serves 8)
12 crabs
2 teaspoons curry powder (optional)
small piece of ginger (crushed)
$\frac{1}{8}$ pint oil
2 tablespoons butter
vinegar or lime juice
salt, to taste
Seasoning (quantities to taste):
1 onion
garlic
cloves
black pepper
hot pepper
chive

3 bay leaves
2 tablespoons rum
1 hot pepper (whole)

flour, for thickening

Method
Keep live crabs in a box for 2 or 3 days, feeding with hot peppers, grass and/or raw, sweet potatoes.

When ready to use, clean the crabs thoroughly, and break in pieces. Remove fat.

Melt butter and crab fat in hot pot. Add crabs, curry powder, seasoning, ginger and oil and allow to stew. Gradually add desired amount of water and bring to the boil with bay leaves, rum and hot pepper.

Add vinegar or lime juice to taste. Thicken slightly.

Crab gumbo

6 crabs
6 ochroes (sliced)
juice of 1 lime
2 tablespoons margarine
cream of 1 grated coconut with water
   made up to 1 pint liquid
salt
Seasoning:
1 onion
1 blade chive
1 clove garlic
1 teaspoon curry powder
4 cloves

Method
Clean crabs and wash thoroughly with lime. Remove fat then break them up.

Melt fat and margarine in hotpot. Add seasoning and sliced ochroes; allow to fry slightly; add crabs. Keep stirring to prevent sticking to pot. Allow to stew for 5 minutes, then add coconut cream. Simmer for 15 minutes. Thicken and add salt as desired.

Periwinkle sancoche

choice of quantity of periwinkle
    (small sea mollusc)
milk of 1 coconut
1 blade chive
1 clove garlic (crushed)
$\frac{1}{2}$ large onion (chopped)
1 sprig thyme
1 tablespoon butter
$\frac{1}{2}$ hot pepper
salt, to taste

flour, to thicken

Method
Wash periwinkles well so that all the
sand is cleaned off, set in cold water
and bring to the boil. Remove the
little black cap from periwinkles.

Grate coconut, add 1 cup water
and extract the milk. Put coconut
milk, chive, garlic, onion, and thyme
to boil with the butter. When it has
come to the boil add periwinkles, salt
and hot pepper. Thicken slightly and
simmer for 5 minutes.

Lambie salad (conch)

(Serves 4)
three lambies (conchs)
4 whole cloves
1 clove garlic (crushed)
onions (juiced)
2 tablespoons oil
2 tablespoons vinegar
salt

parsley
hot pepper (chopped)

Method
Clean and wash lambies thoroughly
with lime until all slime is removed.
Pound until all the tissues are broken.
Place in a bowl with cloves and salt to
taste. Pour boiling water over (enough
to cover lambies) and leave for $\frac{1}{2}$ hr to
1 hour; drain and cut into
small pieces.

Mix together garlic, squeezed
juice of onions, oil and vinegar. Pour
mixture over lambie. Decorate with
parsley and chopped hot pepper.

Curried lambie (conch)

2 lb lambie (conch)
1 lime
$\frac{1}{4}$ cup oil
1 clove garlic (crushed)
2 oz curry powder
1 onion (sliced)
1 sprig celery
1 sprig thyme
1 teaspoon mustard
2 tablespoons margarine or table
　butter
food colouring (if desired)
salt and pepper

Method
Wash conch thoroughly with lime to remove slime. Pound to soften fibres; then dice. Scald or boil in salted water.

　　Heat oil, add garlic, fry. Add curry powder, stir to a paste. Add diced conch, onion, celery, thyme and mustard. Stir to prevent burning. Using water in which the conch was boiled, add sufficient to make a stew. Add salt and pepper to taste. Boil until meat is tender.

　　Add black pepper and margarine (or table butter) to remainder of water to make a broth.

Coubouillon cerique

6 ceriques (fresh water crabs)
1 onion (chopped)
1 tablespoon butter
2 tablespoons oil
1 tablespoon flour
1 pint water
1 hot pepper
bouquet garni
2 tablespoons lime juice
salt

Method
Clean, wash and break ceriques into quarters.

　　Stew onion in butter and oil. Add flour and stir until it forms a roux. Add $\frac{1}{2}$ pint water, stirring all the time.

　　Add cerique and allow to stew for a few minutes. Add remainder of water together with bouquet garni and bring to the boil. Add salt to taste, whole pepper and lime juice. Simmer for 5 minutes.

　　Serve hot with pounded green bananas, green plantains or breadfruit.

Daub cerique

12 ceriques
1 lime (juiced)
3 heads chives
1 green pepper (chopped)
3 whole cloves
garlic (crushed)
1 coconut
1 teaspoon cassareep
salt

Method
Break and wash ceriques. Remove fat. Season with juice of lime, green pepper, cloves, garlic, chives and salt.

Grate coconut, add 1 pint water and squeeze to extract milk.

Put crab to stew in a hotpot with crab fat. Add 1 teaspoon cassareep. Gradually stir in coconut milk. Keep stirring. Allow to cook. When almost cooked, add remainder of milk. Simmer for 10 minutes.

Crayfish coubouilli (Creole)

(Serves 2)
3 crayfish
juice of 1 lime
1 tablespoon margarine
$\frac{1}{2}$ teaspoon chopped parsley
1 clove garlic (crushed)

Method
Clean crayfish thoroughly with lime. Cook in salted boiling water. When cooked cut in halves.

Make a paste of margarine, garlic and parsley.

Place crayfish in a greased dish, spread paste over it and place under a hot grill for 5 minutes.

Turtle stew

3 lb turtle
2 onions (chopped)
2 cloves of garlic (crushed)
1 sprig thyme
2 blades chive
4 tablespoons margarine
$\frac{1}{2}$ cup oil
$\frac{1}{2}$ teaspoon bay leaf seeds or
    6 bay leaves
1 tablespoon flour
vinegar
$\frac{1}{4}$ pint rum
2 tablespoons sugar
10 cloves
salt and pepper

Method
Place turtle in sufficient water to cover, together with 3 bay leaves (or half amount of bay leaf seeds), 5 cloves and salt and pepper to taste and bring to the boil. Remove and set aside 3 cups of the bouillon.

Cut meat in serving pieces; brown in caramelised sugar and hot oil. Add all other ingredients (except the rum and flour) and leave to stew. Slowly add remainder of bouillon and cook until tender.

Add rum, thicken slightly with the flour; simmer for another 5 minutes. Serve hot.

6

Meat

A variety of methods are used in the preparation of meats, for example baking, pot-roasting, roasting over the open fire, grilling, stewing, and the more sophisticated method of barbecuing. The method chosen will, of necessity, depend on the occasion as well as the cut and kind of meat – which may even require elaborate preparation such as stuffing.

Salting and drying meat as a form of preservation is not as widely used as previously, mainly due to the introduction of refrigeration as well as the availability of the commodity at the supermarkets.

However the practice of **smoking** meat, especially pork, is still as popular, to the extent that appropriate-technology workshops have been conducted to introduce housewives to the use of a simple and inexpensive Smoke House.

The secret in cooking meats is the length of time the meat is left in seasoning or to marinate. The meat is marinated hours before cooking and may even be left overnight. In this way the cook is assured that the natural juices are blended with the fresh herbs and liquids (for example: fresh lime juice, vinegar or wine).

The Dominican cook has always baked or roasted meat. Many of the newly-developed recipes require **baking** so this method of cooking has maintained its place in the Dominican kitchen. Furthermore, baking is considered a less time-consuming method of preparing a meal.

Other methods for the Caribs were **baking** their food in the earth and **roasting** the wild game and fish which they caught. This they did over an open fire – over which was erected a grill made of green sticks, known as a galta (see Glossary, page 112). The galta is still found in some of the rural areas.

Barbecuing, which has gained popularity, can be seen as the modernisation of the method practised by the Caribs centuries ago.

Stewing is used for cheaper cuts of meat and for preparing wild game such as agouti, manicou, goat and rabbit.

Pan-fried liver

1 lb liver
1 large onion (sliced)
1 teaspoon vinegar
1 clove garlic (crushed)
2 tablespoons oil
1 tablespoon butter

Method
Dip liver in boiling water for
2 minutes; remove. Take off thin skin.
Slice and cut into cubes.
    Heat oil and butter; add liver and
gradually add about $\frac{1}{2}$ cup water.
Simmer for 15 minutes. Add onion,
garlic and vinegar and simmer for a
further 5 minutes.
    Serve hot.

Grilled liver

1 lb liver
1 large onion (sliced)
4 tablespoons oil
2 tablespoons vinegar
salt
1 teaspoon black pepper
2 large cloves garlic

sliced tomatoes ⎫
lettuce ⎬ to garnish

Method
Scald and skin liver, then slice.
Marinate for 15 minutes in a mixture
(sauce) of vinegar, oil, garlic, salt and
black pepper.
    Heat grill (could be done on an
open fire). Place slices of liver on grill.
Baste with sauce. Keep turning until
cooked as desired.
    Fry onion slices, pour over grilled
liver.
    Serve with tomatoes and lettuce.

Broiled crapaud

(Serves 2)
4 crapauds
Seasoning:
1 onion (grated)
2 cloves garlic (crushed)
1 teaspoon salt
$\frac{1}{2}$ teaspoon black pepper
1 tablespoon Lea & Perrins Sauce
1 sprig thyme
2 heads chive (mashed)
1 sprig celery (mashed)
2 eggs
2 oz margarine or shortening

Method
Stand crapaud in the blended mixture
of all the other ingredients (except the
margarine) for 30 minutes.
    Place sauté pan to heat, then melt
margarine. Pour crapaud and
seasoning mixture into pan. Simmer
for 15 minutes, stirring every
5 minutes. Season with salt and
pepper to taste.
    Serve garnished with parsley.

Preparing 'mountain chicken' (frog) for dinner

Fricassé mountain chicken (crapaud)

3 crapauds (Dominica frogs)
1 lime
$\frac{1}{8}$pint oil
2 oz margarine
2 teaspoons vinegar
1 tablespoon ketchup
2 oz flour
1$\frac{1}{2}$cups water
Seasoning:
onion (chopped)
garlic (crushed)
cloves
salt and black pepper } to taste
thyme
celery

Method
Clean and cut up crapauds into
pieces. Wash thoroughly with lime.
Sprinkle with a teaspoon vinegar, salt,
pepper, chopped onion and garlic.
Marinate in this seasoning for 1 hour
then remove and dry. Roll each piece
in flour and fry until golden brown.

Melt margarine in hotpot. Add
the remainder of the seasoning, then
allow to sauté. Add fried crapaud,
then water. Simmer for 5 minutes.
Add 1 teaspoon vinegar, ketchup, salt
and pepper to taste. Thicken if
desired. Simmer for a further
5 minutes before serving.

Curried goat

1 quarter goat
2 large onions
4 oz curry powder
4 blades chive
1 sprig each of parsley and thyme
1 small bottle ketchup
Lea & Perrins sauce
4 cloves garlic (crushed)
vinegar
salt and black pepper
4 bay leaves
1 hot pepper
2 tablespoons sugar (for colouring)
$\frac{1}{8}$pint oil
2 tablespoons flour (for thickening)

Method
Cut meat into serving pieces. Chop
1 onion, chives, parsley, thyme,
2 cloves garlic and add to mixture of
vinegar, salt, black pepper, dash of
Lea & Perrins Sauce, $\frac{1}{2}$bottle ketchup,
2 oz curry powder. Marinate meat
overnight in mixture.

Heat an iron pot, add oil, allow
to heat. Add sugar. Let sugar and oil
burn to make colouring. Pour in meat,
allow to brown. Add liquid in which
meat was marinated and enough
water to cover the meat. Bring to the
boil. Add remaining curry powder.
Boil until meat is tender. Season to
taste with balance of ingredients.
Thicken slightly. Simmer for
10 minutes.

Serve with rice.

Suckling pig

suckling pig prepared for baking
salt, pepper, vinegar, garlic
1 orange, onion or apple
Stuffing:
2 bundles chives
2 sprigs thyme
1 bundle parsley
2 large onions
$\frac{1}{4}$*lb bacon*
1 hot pepper

blood of pig
2 teaspoons seasoning salt
dash of Angostura Bitters
dash of Lea & Perrins sauce
2 tablespoons tomato ketchup
$\frac{1}{8}$*pint oil*
4 teaspoons butter

Method
Wipe pig thoroughly inside and outside with cloth dampened in vinegar. Rub inside and outside with salt and garlic. Set aside.

Method
Cut up chive, bacon, thyme, parsley, onion, hot pepper. Allow oil to heat and add chopped seasoning; fry gently. Remove pot from fire and allow to cool. Add blood of pig, stirring constantly to prevent curdling. Add the remainder of the ingredients.

When the mixture is cold, fill the cavity or belly of the pig. Stuff the mouth with orange, onion or apple. Sew up or close up with skewers. Very lightly smear the outside with butter.

Bake in moderate oven basting frequently.

Game

Stewed manicou *A la Sisserou Hotel*

2 prepared manicou
$\frac{1}{2}$ lb carrots (sliced)
4 oz onions (sliced)
4 oz pepper (sliced)
4 tablespoons margarine
1 cup water
vinegar
1 clove garlic (crushed)
salt and pepper

Method
Cut manicou into quarters. Marinate in mixture of vinegar, salt, pepper, and garlic. Leave to stand for 3 hours.

Heat oven to 450 °F. Remove meat from seasoning. Place in a casserole. Spread carrots, onions and sweet pepper over meat. Dot over with margarine. Add water and salt to taste. Cover tightly and cook in oven for 1 hour.

Stewed agouti *A la Sisserou Hotel*

(As above using two prepared agouti in place of manicou.)

Stewed ramier

6 ramier
2 large onions (chopped)
2 cloves garlic
1 sprig thyme
3 blades chive
$\frac{1}{2}$ teaspoon bay leaf seeds (pounded)
vinegar
2 sprigs celery (chopped)
2 tablespoons white pepper
salt

1 clove garlic
2 tablespoons brown sugar
1 tablespoon flour
$\frac{1}{2}$ cup oil

Preparation
Feather and cut bird down the centre and clean properly. Prepare a marinade from vinegar, chive, garlic, onions, thyme, bay leaf seeds, celery, sufficient water for the birds to be submerged, salt and pepper to taste. Marinate birds overnight.

Pour oil into hotpot. Allow the sugar to caramelise in oil; add 1 clove of garlic and allow to fry.

Remove meat from the marinade. Add to the hotpot and allow to brown, stirring constantly. Add seasoned water when meat is properly browned. Boil until tender. Thicken with flour and water. Season to taste and simmer for 10 minutes.

Serve with pounded green plantains and red beans or pigeon peas.

Note: Manicou and agouti may also be prepared and stewed in the same manner as described for ramier.

Smoked meat

(Serves 6)
fine salt
pepper (pounded)
green banana leaves

Method
Gash meat all over to open up flat and to enable salt to penetrate. Rub fine salt, pounded pepper into gashes.

Place meat in an earthenware container or any other suitable container. Cover and leave for 3 to 4 days to allow salt to penetrate and the water to be extracted.

Remove excess salt from the meat and drain.

The prepared meat is then placed on a *boucan* with the salted section towards the fire and covered with green banana leaves for about 3 days.

When the meat is finished it should be golden brown. Meat smoked in this manner will last for months.

Glazed pot with wooden cover, used for pickling meat

7

Staple starchy foods

Breadfruit gratin

(Serves 6)
1 breadfruit
2 eggs
1 cup milk
1½ cups grated cheese
salt and pepper, to taste

¼ cup breadcrumbs
2 tablespoons butter

Method
Peel and dice breadfruit. Boil until tender. Drain and leave to cool.

Mix the beaten egg, milk, ½ cup grated cheese salt and pepper. Add to breadfruit. Pour into greased casserole dish. Spread 1 cup grated cheese over mixture. Cover with breadcrumbs. Dot with butter.

Bake in oven 350–400 °F for 45 minutes.

Breadfruit cheese

1 breadfruit
6 oz cheese (grated)
1 pint milk
2 tablespoons margarine
2 tablespoons flour
salt and pepper, to taste
1 onion (sliced)

margarine, as necessary

Method
Steam breadfruit and slice thinly. Lay slices one on top of the other in a greased dish.

Prepare a thin cheese sauce with balance of ingredients, leaving 2 tablespoons grated cheese for topping. Pour sauce over the breadfruit, making sure it is properly covered with the sauce. Sprinkle cheese on top.

Dot with margarine and bake in a moderate oven until golden brown.

Creamed-breadfruit pie

Breadfruit and sweetcorn pie

For recipes, see page 105.

Roast breadfruit

1 breadfruit

Method
Put whole breadfruit over the flame of an open fire. Keep turning until breadfruit becomes lighter and is soft to the touch. When cooked either scrape top skin off or peel.

Serve with cucumber salad and roasted codfish.

Breadfruit flour

1 breadfruit

Method

Peel breadfruit, and core. Cut into thin slices, then put to dry. When thoroughly dried out slices will be hard. Pound in a mortar, then sift.

Flour can be used to make dumplings or cake.

Daub yampain (stewed breadfruit)

1 breadfruit
1 onion (sliced)
1 clove garlic (crushed)
2 tablespoons butter
2 tablespoons cooking oil
salt and pepper

Method

Peel breadfruit. Slice and pack in a saucepan. Add sufficient water to cover the bottom of the pan. Add onion, garlic, salt and pepper to taste. Bring to the boil.

When the breadfruit is cooked add butter and cooking oil. Simmer for 3 minutes.

Serve with fried chicken or fried fish.

Pain doux (sweet corn bread)

4 pints fresh corn (ground)
1 large coconut
1 lb sugar
2 teaspoons vanilla essence
1 piece cinnamon

young banana leaves

Method

Sift corn.

Grate coconut and extract milk, adding enough water to make up 2 pints of milk. Bring coconut milk to the boil adding sugar, vanilla and cinnamon. Remove from fire and allow to cool. Mix with ground corn.

Blanche banana leaves either in hot water or over the fire. With a rolling pin shape leaves into a cylinder. Tie one end with corn straw.

Fill leaf-cylinder with mixture and secure other end by tying. When all the mixture is used up, cook in boiling, salted water for 50 minutes.

Coco macaque (corn dumpling) (1)

4 pints fresh corn (ground)
1 large coconut
2 pints water
2 oz margarine
1 clove garlic (crushed)
salt and pepper, to taste

young banana leaves

Method
Sift corn.

Grate coconut and extract milk, adding enough water to make up 2 pints of milk. Bring coconut milk to the boil together with garlic, margarine, salt and pepper. Remove from fire and allow to cool. Mix with ground corn.

Blanche banana leaves either in hot water or over the fire. With a rolling pin shape leaves into a cylinder. Tie one end with corn straw.

Fill leaf-cylinder with mixture and secure other end by tying. When all the mixture is used up, cook in boiling, salted water for 50 minutes.

Coco macaque (2)

4 fresh ears of corn (minced and
    sifted)
1 lb flour
1 coconut (grated)
1 blade chive (chopped)
1 oz butter
1 onion (grated)
1 clove garlic (crushed)

Method
Extract milk from coconut with $\frac{1}{2}$ pint water and put to boil with butter, chive, onion and garlic.

Mix flour and corn. Add boiled milk gradually to dry ingredients. When mixture is stiff to stir set aside to cool.

Spoon cooled mixture into salted, boiling water to which the water of the coconut may be added. Boil for 15 minutes, stirring occasionally to prevent dumplings from sticking together.

Coco macaque (3)

12 large green corns (ground)
2 teaspoons salt
1 cup lukewarm water

Method
Mix all ingredients adding water gradually until it forms into a hard dough. Form into dumplings.

Cook in salted, boiling water for 15 minutes.

Pain mie (corn bread)

1 lb fresh green corn (ground)
1 lb sugar
1 cup milk or coconut milk
½ teaspoon nutmeg
2 teaspoons vanilla essence

banana leaves (singed)

Method
Mix all ingredients except banana leaves to a dropping consistency. Add water if necessary. Fill banana leaves with about two tablespoons of the mixture. Fold and tie securely.
   Cook for about 1 hour in salted water.

Plantain (boiled in African sauce)

4 or 5 firm ripe plantains
sweet peppers (green and red, sliced)
1 onion (sliced)
1 tablespoon margarine
1 dash Lea & Perrins Sauce
1 teaspoon prepared mustard
tomato ketchup, to taste

Method
Boil plantains and slice lengthwise.
   In ½ cup water place all other ingredients and leave to simmer (African sauce). Pour over plantains.
   Serve hot.

Stuffed yams

(Serves 6)
1 medium-size ladies yam (3 lb)
2 oz bacon (chopped)
2 oz chicken liver (chopped)
1 head chive (chopped)
1 onion (chopped)
½ cup milk
2 tablespoons margarine

Method
Peel yam and cut lengthwise. Boil in salted water until tender. Drain carefully to avoid breaking and leave to cool. Scoop out centre of yam leaving a shell of 1″ in depth. Mash scooped-out yam.
   Sauté bacon, liver, chive and onion in margarine. Add crushed yam and milk. Mix thoroughly. Fill yam shell with mixture. Place under a hot grill until brown.
   Serve as main dish.

Pounding

It is in the preparation of root tubers, commonly referred to as ground provisions, that the Dominican cuisine has one of its direct links with the West African culture. The slaves who were allowed to cultivate their own kitchen gardens not only introduced their own food, but practised the method of cooking they knew. One method of serving staples such as breadfruit, plantains, green bananas or dasheen, is to pound them in a wooden mortar with a wooden pestle known as a *manch pillon*.

Ton-ton, as the pounded food is called, is an adaptation of *foo-foo*, cooked and crushed yam, cassava or plantain, found in West African cuisine.

Plantain – pounded

green plaintains (quantity as required)

Method
Peel plaintains and cook in salted, boiling water. Pound in a wooden mortar, adding small quantities of water while pounding, until mixture is gummy.

Serve with fish coubouillon or codfish coubouillon and pigeon peas.

All the ingredients for pounded plantain

Farine

cassava (quantity as required – one large root should yield $\frac{1}{2}$ pint farine)

Method

To make farine, scrape and grate cassava, pour the wet husk into a bag and place under a press to remove the poisonous juice. Sift the husk through a bamboo strainer. Dry out husk in a well-heated iron pot, constantly stirring to prevent burning. When dried out sufficiently, store in a bag or tin.

Farine can be eaten mixed with avocado pear, grated dry coconut, peas, cocoa, fish *or* meat gravy or titiri.

Farine can also be eaten as a cereal.

Farine (Carib)

Cook farine (see above) in boiling, salted water until hard.

Serve with fish or meat.

Sugar-boiling taché used here for baking cassava farine

Sylvia

8

One-pot dishes

Sancoche (broth)

2 lb pickled meat
2 onions (sliced)
1 blade chive
2 tablespoons butter
$\frac{1}{8}$ pint oil
1 green pepper
1 clove garlic (crushed)
milk from 1 coconut
$\frac{1}{2}$ lb yam
$\frac{1}{2}$ lb dasheen
$\frac{1}{2}$ lb green bananas
2 green plantains
$\frac{1}{2}$ lb tannias
salt, to taste

Method
Put meat to boil in 6 pints water.
When meat is almost cooked, peel
yam, dasheen, green bananas, green
plantains and tannias and cut into
pieces of required size. Add to pot and
boil for 20 minutes. Add all other
ingredients and simmer for a further
20 minutes.

Flour dumplings

1 cup flour
$\frac{1}{4}$ teaspoon salt

Method
Sift flour and salt together and slowly
add sufficient cold water to make a
stiff dough. Knead in the bowl or on a
lightly-floured board until texture is
smooth.

Cut dough into equally-sized
pieces, form into balls, then press flat
or roll. Bring salted water to boil and
add dough pieces. Boil for 15 to
20 minutes.
Note: To make **Droppers** ensure the
mixture is sufficiently soft to drop
from a spoon.

Crab pelau

4 crabs
1 lb rice
4 cups coconut milk (see Glossary,
　page 112)
3 tablespoons oil
1 tablespoons curry powder
1 onion (chopped)
1 clove garlic (crushed)
bouquet garni
4½ cups water

Method
Clean crabs and break up into pieces
– reserving fat for frying.
　Fry onion in hot oil and fat from
crab. Add curry powder, bouquet
garni, garlic and crab and allow to
stew. Add coconut milk and water;
simmer for 30 minutes.
　Add rice, reduce heat and cook
until rice is soft.

Bouquet garni

Chicken pelau

3–4 lb chicken
4 cups rice
10 cups water
1 cup peas or beans
2 tablespoons Lea & Perrins sauce
2 tablespoons sugar
2 tablespoons oil
2 tablespoons butter
1 dash Angostura Bitters
1 small bottle tomato ketchup
Seasoning:
1 sweet pepper
2 blades chive
1 sprig thyme
2 cloves garlic
2 onions
1 hot pepper
1 sprig celery
1 sprig parsley

Method
Soak peas or beans overnight. Next
day boil until tender, then remove
from heat.
　Cut chicken into pieces; season
with salt, pepper and Lea & Perrins
sauce. Fry in burnt sugar and oil until
golden brown.
　Chop all seasonings and sauté in
butter, ketchup and Bitters. Pour
sauté mixture over browned chicken
and allow to marinate.
　Place water in pot; add chicken
and bring to the boil. Add rice and
peas and lower heat. Cook until rice is
soft. Do not allow contents to become
dry.

Braf (broth)

(Serves 6)
1 lb pickled or *smoked pork*
1 lb sprats or *small jacks*
½ lb dasheen
½ lb tannias
½ lb green bananas
2 medium christophines
1 lb cabbage
⅛ pint oil
Seasoning:
juice of 2 green limes
2 blades chive
1 sprig thyme
2 cloves garlic
1 onion (chopped)
1 hot pepper
3 cloves

Clay pot and egg-plant

Method
Soak meat to remove some of the salt. Clean fish and put in water, salt, to taste, 1 clove crushed garlic and juice of one lime, sufficient to cover the fish. Set aside.

Now peel and wash the ground provisions and cut into serving portions. Peel and slice christophines. Cut cabbage into four sections.

Drain meat and boil until almost tender. Add vegetables and ground provisions to pot. When almost cooked add seasoned fish and remaining seasoning. Simmer.

Add oil and serve hot.

Pomkia (Carib)

$\frac{1}{2}$*lb each of dasheen, tannia,*
    pumpkin, pawpaw, yam
1 coconut
any quantity fish or crayfish
salt, to taste
Seasoning (quantities as required):
chive
celery
garlic
parsley
cloves

Method
Thoroughly clean fish. Peel and wash
provisions and either cut into small
pieces or grate.

Grate coconut and extract milk
using enough water to cover
provisions in pot. Add seasoning and
salt. Place fish in pot and cover. Boil
until milk is almost absorbed, then
remove pot from heat. Carefully
remove fish and remove all bones.
If provisions have not been grated
remove pieces from pot and crush
with boneless fish until mixture
resembles a paste. Return to pot
and place on fire to simmer for
10 minutes. Serve hot.

Cook-up rice

$1\frac{1}{2}$*lb chicken (back and neck)*
$\frac{1}{2}$*lb pig tail or salt beef (chopped)*
1 lb rice
1 small coconut
$\frac{1}{2}$*lb pigeon peas (or beans)*
2 tablespoons cooking oil
1–2 onions (chopped)
2 heads chive (chopped)
1 large tomato
salt and pepper

oil, for frying

Method
Soak peas or beans overnight.

Next day, cut up chicken back
and neck and season with onion,
chive, tomato, salt and pepper. Set
aside for 1 hour.

Grate coconut and extract milk
with 1 pint of water.

Bring $2\frac{1}{2}$ pints water to the boil;
add peas. Cook until soft or burst.
Strain and save water (stock).

Heat oil in pot, add back and
neck and pig tail. Fry until brown.
Add all seasonings and stir
thoroughly. Add peas and rice to pot,
then the stock saved and coconut
milk. Stir and cook over low heat
until rice is tender and liquid is
absorbed.

9

Desserts

Coconut jelly

1 coconut (grated)
1 tin evaporated milk + equal amount
    of water
3 oz gelatine powder
6 tablespoons hot water
sugar, as required
1 dash Angostura Bitters
1 teaspoon almond essence
Topping:
1 cup grated coconut
$\frac{1}{2}$ cup sugar

Method
Heat milk and pour over grated
coconut. Leave to stand for $\frac{1}{2}$ hour,
then strain. Pour equal amount of
water over coconut hash and extract
all milk.

Dissolve gelatine in hot water
and add to milk extract. Sweeten to
taste. Add dash of Bitters and essence.
Pour into a dish or individual serving
glasses. Chill until set.

Top with grated coconut which
has been browned with sugar in pan
over fire.

Plantain custard

3 over-ripe plantains
$\frac{3}{4}$ pint evaporated milk
2 eggs
2 tablespoons sugar
rind of 1 lime
1 teaspoon nutmeg

Method
Peel and slice plantains. Lay in a
greased dish.

Make custard with eggs, milk
and sugar, add lime rind and whip
together. Pour over plantains, top
with nutmeg and bake until firm and
plantains are cooked.

78

Sweet potato pudding (1)

2 lb sweet potatoes
1 teaspoon salt
2 lb sugar
milk of 1 grated coconut (using
   2 pints water)
2 oz green ginger (grated)
2–4 oz corn meal (if desired)

Method
Peel, wash and grate sweet potatoes.
Mix in salt, coconut milk and ginger
thoroughly. If texture is too soft add
small quantities of corn meal until
desired texture is achieved. Pour into
a buttered pan and bake in a low oven
until firm.

Sweet potato pudding (2)

2 large sweet potatoes
1 teaspoon grated ginger
1 teaspoon mixed spice
1 tin evaporated milk
2 eggs
2 teaspoons vanilla essence
sugar, to taste

Method
Peel, wash and grate sweet potatoes;
add ginger.
   Add enough water to milk to
make 1 pint. Beat together eggs and
milk to make a custard; add to potato
and ginger mixture. Stir, adding
mixed spice, essence and sugar to
taste.
   Pour into a buttered dish and
bake in a low oven until firm. Remove
from oven and allow to cool, then cut
into squares.

Sweet potato pudding (3)

2 lb sweet potatoes
1 teaspoon each of grated ginger,
   nutmeg and spice
$\frac{1}{2}$ coconut (grated)
2 ripe bananas (mashed)
2 teaspoons vanilla essence
grated rind of 2 limes
1 level teaspoon black pepper
2 oz raisins (optional)
$\frac{1}{2}$ pint syrup (home-made or
prepared)
water, as required

Method
Peel, wash and grate sweet potatoes.
Mix remaining ingredients well and
add to grated potatoes. If required
add sufficient water to form a
dropping consistency.
   Pour mixture into a buttered pan,
top with dots of butter and bake in a
low oven until firm.

Kankey (Carib)

cassava, enough to give 2 pints when
  grated
$\frac{1}{2}$ pint water
1 lb sugar
2 teaspoons cinnamon
1 grated nutmeg
grated rind of 1 lime
1 teaspoon vanilla essence

2 tablespoons sugar
banana leaves (singed)

Method
Squeeze out bitter water from grated
cassava. Mix all other ingredients to a
syrup made with sugar and water; add
to grated cassava. Mix thoroughly;
then roll into lengths of about 4".
Place each roll on singed banana leaf
and make a parcel by folding. Add
2 tablespoons sugar to water in pot
and bring to the boil. Place parcels in
pot making sure water is sufficient to
cover all parcels. Allow to boil for
75 minutes.

Coconut sherbert

2 coconuts (dried coconut can be used
  if desired)
1 tin condensed milk
vanilla or almond essence
jelly of coconut if not using dried
  coconut

Method
Squeeze out milk from coconut if
using dried coconut. Otherwise use
coconut water and, if desired, use jelly
also.
     Mix all ingredients together,
place in ice tray and freeze.

Banana trifle

1-day-old sponge cake
ripened bananas (quantity as
  required)
juice of 1 large lime
jelly or jam of choice
sherry, wine or brandy
custard (home-made or prepared)

Method
Cut cake into $\frac{1}{4}$" slices. Line bottom
of buttered baking pan with them.
Place slices of ripe bananas dipped in
lime juice over cake. Sprinkle with
choice of sherry, wine or brandy.
Place a layer of jelly (or jam) and
place a second layer of cake.
     If desired, sprinkle again with
choice of sherry, wine or brandy and
top with custard.
     Chill and serve.

Banana snow

2 ripe bananas (mashed)
$\frac{1}{4}$ cup lemon juice
whites of 2 eggs
1 tablespoon gelatine (softened)
$\frac{1}{4}$ cup cold water
1 teaspoon grated lemon rind
$\frac{3}{4}$ cup sugar
$\frac{1}{4}$ teaspoon salt
1 cup hot water

Method
Mix together the sugar, salt, water and lemon rind. Add softened gelatine and stir until dissolved. Now add lemon juice and chill until partially set.

Next stir in two mashed bananas. Beat egg whites with a whisk until frothy then fold into mixture. Pour into mould and chill until firm.

If desired, unmould before serving. Can also be served with a custard sauce.

Servants' quarters on the old plantation

Home-made ice cream

Basic ice-cream

3 tins evaporated milk
2 tins condensed milk
2 tablespoons custard powder
½ teaspoon vanilla essence
sugar (if desired)

Method
Add enough water to evaporated milk to make 3 pints. Using 2 tablespoons milk soften custard powder.

Bring evaporated milk to the boil and gradually stir in custard powder. Allow to boil until thickened, stirring constantly to prevent sticking or burning. Add remaining ingredients to boiling mixture, continuing to stir. Allow to boil for another 5 minutes. Remove from heat, cool and freeze.

Note: This is the basic mixture (or custard) for the following varieties of ice-cream. It is recommended that ice-cream tubs or similar containers be used for freezing.

If desired, to attain a smooth soft texture to ice-cream after freezing in the freezer compartment of the fridge, blend or whisk briskly for about 15 seconds, replace in freezer and allow to harden.

Fruits in abundance

Flavour varieties for home-made ice-cream

1 Coconut ice-cream

To basic mixture:
before freezing, add 1 pint coconut milk and, if desired, add sugar. Whisk or blend briskly for 15 seconds. Freeze.

2 Pineapple ice-cream

To basic mixture:
when custard begins to harden add crushed canned pineapple or pineapple jam; whisk briskly for 15 seconds and return to complete freezing, if not made in an ice-cream tub.

3 Soursop ice-cream

To basic mixture:
before freezing, add juice of 1 soursop. (To extract soursop juice pour $1\frac{1}{2}$ cups hot water over seedless pulp or soursop fruit and allow to stand for 1 hour. Liquidise with blender, or squeeze juice through a sieve.) Freeze.

4 Barbadine ice-cream

To basic mixture:
before freezing cut and squeeze barbadine; add juice and fruit seeds, blend into custard and freeze.

5 Guava ice-cream

To basic mixture:
when custard begins to harden add guava either mashed or cut into small pieces. Complete freezing. (Guava jam may be used instead of fresh guavas.)

6 Strawberry ice-cream

To basic mixture:
when custard begins to harden add strawberries either mashed or cut into small pieces. Complete freezing. (Strawberry jam may be used instead of fresh strawberries.)

Banana ice-cream

1 cup water
$\frac{1}{2}$ cup powdered milk
$\frac{1}{2}$ cup sugar
2 teaspoons vanilla essence
2 ripe bananas

Method
Blend all ingredients together until liquidised. Continue to blend for a further 3 minutes. Place into dish and freeze for 1 hour.

This dessert can be served just as it is – frozen or, to achieve a smooth texture, can be blended at high speed for 1 minute before placing in individual serving glasses.

10

Breads, cakes and pastries

Breads

Jackerie (Biscuit bread)

3 oz dry yeast
$\frac{1}{2}$ bag flour
1 gallon water
1 lb salt

Method
Dissolve yeast in warm water. Mix flour and salt with this yeast mixture. Leave to rise until double its original bulk.

Pass through jackerie machine until dough becomes smooth. Cut dough with jackerie cutter to required size.

Bake immediately in medium (stone) oven for 30–40 minutes.

Cassava bread

2 pints farine (see page 73)
$\frac{1}{2}$ coconut (grated)
salt, to taste

Method
Stir in salt and coconut with farine. Mix thoroughly. Bake in a hot iron pot, shaping into round biscuits with a wooden spoon. Allow to brown on one side then turn and brown other side.

Serve with cocoa as a breakfast meal.

Garlic bread

4 *cloves garlic*
4 *oz table butter*
bread slices

Method
Blend together butter and crushed garlic to make a spread. Butter each bread slice thoroughly.

Place on cookie sheet in a hot oven until butter has melted.

Keep warm by wrapping in tin foil until ready to serve.

Bakes

1 *cup flour*
$\frac{1}{4}$ *teaspoon salt*
1 $\frac{1}{2}$ *teaspoons baking powder*
1 *tablespoon margarine*
milk, as required

cooking oil

Method
Sift flour, baking powder and salt together. Rub in margarine. Slowly add enough milk to make a stiff dough. Turn dough on to a lightly-floured board and knead until smooth. Cut dough and shape into equal-sized balls.

Heat oil in pan. Flatten dough balls and fry evenly on both sides until golden brown. Serve warm.

Cakes

Coconut cookies

1 lb flour
4 oz brown sugar
1 heaped tablespoon baking powder
4 oz margarine
1 cup milk
1 coconut (grated)
1 tablespoon essence (cinnamon)
1 egg

Method
Sift flour, sugar and baking powder together. Rub margarine into sifted mixture. Make a hole in centre of mixture and break egg into hole, stirring vigorously. Add essence.

Place in small heaps on greased cookie sheet and flatten to shape. Bake in oven at 375°F for 15 minutes or until golden brown.

Coconut drops

3 cups flour
$\frac{1}{2}$ cup margarine
1 cup sugar
3 tablespoons baking powder
2 coconuts (grated)
1 teaspoon vanilla or almond essence
2 eggs

Method
Mix all ingredients together. Place in small heaps on cookie sheet. Bake in oven at 375°F for 40 minutes.

Makes 30.

Pewyer

4 lb flour
2 pints syrup
1 piece ginger (crushed)
2 heaped tablespoons baking soda
1 tablespoon nutmeg
1 tablespoon spice (cinnamon)
$\frac{1}{2}$ pint water

Method
Mix together baking soda, ginger, nutmeg, spice and water. Pour mixture into syrup and stir thoroughly. Add flour and knead into a soft dough.

On a lightly-floured board roll out the dough and cut it into strips. Roll strips of dough using palms of hands and make like a long rope. Coil into a round shape.

Place each coil on a greased cookie (or tin) sheet and bake in a moderate oven for 15–20 minutes.

Nutmeg: mace nut and grater

Cross cakes

4 lb flour
2 pints syrup
1 piece ginger (crushed)
2 heaped tablespoons baking soda
1 tablespoon nutmeg
1 tablespoon spice (cinnamon)
$\frac{1}{2}$ pint water

Method
Mix together baking soda, ginger, nutmeg, spice and water. Pour mixture into syrup and stir thoroughly. Add flour and knead into a soft dough.

On a lightly-floured board roll out the dough and cut into oblong pieces with a dough cutter. Place on a greased cookie (or tin) sheet and bake in a moderate oven for 15–20 minutes.

Belbo

4 lb flour
2 pints syrup
1 piece ginger (crushed)
2 heaped tablespoons baking soda
1 tablespoon nutmeg
1 tablespoon spice (cinnamon)
$\frac{1}{2}$ pint water

Method
Mix together baking soda, ginger, nutmeg, spice and water. Pour mixture into syrup and stir thoroughly. Add flour and knead into a soft dough.

Drop mixture by spoonfuls on to a greased cookie (or tin) sheet and bake in a moderate oven for 15–20 minutes.

Rough cake

1 lb flour
$\frac{3}{4}$ lb brown sugar
4 tablespoons grated coconut
$\frac{1}{2}$ oz baking powder
1 teaspoon mixed spice
$\frac{1}{2}$ pint water

Method
Make a syrup with water and sugar. Add to flour, baking powder and spice. Add coconut.

Place mixture by spoonfuls on to a greased cookie (or tin) sheet and bake in a moderate oven for 30–40 minutes or until golden brown.

Pumpkin cake

8 oz flour
$\frac{1}{2}$ cup uncooked pumpkin (grated)
6 oz sugar
4 oz butter
2 eggs
2 teaspoons baking powder
1 teaspoon grated lime rind
1 teaspoon almond essence
$\frac{1}{2}$ teaspoon salt
$\frac{1}{2}$ cup milk

Method
Separate yolks from whites of egg.

Cream together butter and sugar. Beat egg yolks one at a time into creamed mixture. Now add the grated lime rind.

Sift together flour, baking powder and salt. Little by little add alternately with milk to creamed mixture. Add essence and fold in grated pumpkin.

Beat egg whites until stiff and fold into mixture. Pour into greased baking pan and bake in a moderate oven (375°F) until firm.

Arrowroot cake

$\frac{1}{2}$ *cup flour*
2 cups arrowroot
1 cup sugar
7 oz shortening
2 egg yolks
grated rind of lime
1 teaspoon vanilla essence
1 teaspoon almond essence
$\frac{1}{2}$ *cup water*

Method
Boil water and sugar with spices to make a light syrup. Mix arrowroot and flour and make a hole in centre. Add syrup, egg yolks, shortening and essence and form into a dough ball. Roll out dough and cut into desired shape(s). Bake in a hot oven at 400 °F until firm.

Vanilla: the vine, bloom, cured pod and bottled extract

Christmas cake (fruit cake)

2 lb flour (sifted)
1 lb sugar
1 lb butter
12 eggs
8 oz glacé cherries (chopped)
8 oz mixed peel
2 teaspoons allspice
½ teaspoon grated nutmeg
2 tablespoons vanilla essence
2 tablespoons almond essence
2 tablespoons stout (optional)
grated rind of one lemon or *lime*
food browning or *caramelised sugar*
½ bottle sweet red wine

Preparation (at least one month before baking)
1 lb raisins
1 lb currants } *finely chopped or minced*
8 oz prunes
Soak mixture in 1½ bottles sweet red wine

Method
Preheat oven to 425 °F. Grease and line two 8″ cake pans.

Cream butter and sugar; gradually add beaten eggs and lemon rind. Beat thoroughly. Now, stirring continuously, add the cherries, mixed peel, wine-soaked fruit, essence, spice, nutmeg, stout (if desired), caramelised sugar or food browning and blend thoroughly. If a darker coloured cake is required then add more caramelised sugar/food browning. Finally, fold in the flour.

Pour mixture into prepared pans. Cook for 15 minutes at 425°F then reduce oven temperature to 300°F and bake cake for a further 1–2 hours. Test by piercing with a toothpick: if it comes away clean then the cakes are ready to be removed from the oven. Pour ½ bottle of wine over cakes and leave to cool. Once cooled, wrap them in greaseproof paper, then foil to retain moisture.

These cakes can last up to 1 year. If desired, periodically pour liquor on top to maintain softness.

Pastries

Basic pastry dough

1 lb flour
2 oz butter
2 oz lard (shortening)
2 oz water

Method
Rub in butter and lard with flour.
Add sufficient water to form a dough.
Roll dough thinly on a lightly-floured board. Cut into squares (or other desired shapes) and use as a shell for various fillings.

Paté banan

1 oz lard
plantains (bananas), as necessary

basic pastry (as above)

Method
Using basic pastry recipe add an additional 1 oz lard to pastry mixture.
Roll out pastry dough into a square. Using over-ripe plantains, slice and place slices in centre of pastry square. Fold over both ends, place on a greased cookie sheet and bake in a hot oven for 10 minutes.

Paté coco

1 coconut (grated)
1 lb sugar
1 teaspoon almond essence
2 pints water

basic pastry (as above)

Method
Boil coconut together with sugar in water. Stir constantly until mixture leaves sides of saucepan. Add almond essence.
Using basic pastry roll out and cut into circle shapes. Spoon coconut mixture on to $\frac{1}{2}$ of pastry circle and flip over other half of circle. Pinch edges together for sealing in filling.
Bake in a hot oven for 10 minutes.

11

Confectionery

Candied potatoes

6 *sweet potatoes*
$\frac{1}{2}$ *cup butter*
1 *cup brown sugar*
1 *teaspoon powdered cinnamon*
$\frac{1}{2}$ *cup water*

Method
Boil potatoes before peeling, then peel and slice.

Melt butter and sugar in frying pan. Add powdered cinnamon and water. Add cooked potato slices and allow to simmer for a few minutes.

Remove from pan and place in a pyrex dish. Sprinkle lightly with brown sugar and a dusting of cinnamon. Dot with butter. Place in a moderate oven for 10–15 minutes.

Caramel bananas

6 *firm ripe bananas*
$\frac{3}{4}$ *cup brown sugar (lightly packed)*
2 *tablespoons melted margarine* or *butter*
$\frac{1}{3}$ *cup raisins*
$\frac{1}{3}$ *cup water*

Method
Peel and cut bananas lengthwise in half. Place in a skillet or large, flat, frying pan. Sprinkle with sugar and melted margarine (or butter). Add raisins to pan. Cover with water. Cook over low heat until bananas are tender, brushing frequently with the syrup.

Serve warm with coconut ice-cream.

Confetti potatoes (sweet potato jam)

2 cups sweet potatoes (diced)
juice of 1 lime
2 cups sugar
1 cup water
1 vanilla pod
$\frac{1}{4}$ teaspoon grated nutmeg

Method
Peel and wash potatoes with water to which lime juice has been added. Dice potatoes. Boil together with nutmeg, and vanilla and 1 cup water over low fire. Allow to boil until potatoes are tender and syrupy.

Shaddock preserves

1 shaddock
2 lb sugar
1 cup water

Method
Cut shaddock into quarters. Peel off rind and discard with inside of fruit; scald by pouring boiling water over white flesh. Squeeze to remove water and put to soak in cold water for 2 hours.

Prepare a syrup with water and sugar.

Squeeze water from shaddock by gently twisting. Now lay slices in the syrup. Allow to simmer on low heat until liquid becomes very thick. Remove shaddock slices and lay flat in a dish. Sprinkle with sugar and allow to cool.

Will become hard when cool.

Farine coco

1 coconut (grated)
$\frac{1}{2}$ cup sugar

Method
Squeeze milk out of coconut (save milk for making coconut cheese). Mix coconut with sugar.

Place mixture in a pre-heated pot over moderate fire and parch, stirring constantly to prevent burning. When husk becomes dried out remove from fire; leave to cool and then parcel into paper packets.

Coconut cheese

1 coconut (grated)
1 lb sugar
1 teaspoon essence (cinnamon)

Method
Squeeze milk out of coconut, mix milk with sugar. Put to boil until sugar crystals appear around edge of saucepan. Add essence and grated coconut.

Remove from heat and beat until mixture thickens. Pour into greased moulds or over marble top. Will harden when cool. Cut into squares.

Coconut cake (coconut sweet)

3 cups coconut (grated)
3 cups sugar
1 small piece ginger
1 small piece cinnamon
1 teaspoon essence (cinnamon)
1 cup water

Method
Boil sugar and water slowly to form a thin syrup. Add grated coconut, whole cinnamon and ginger. Cook until syrup dries and crystals appear around the saucepan.

Remove from heat, stir well, remove the cinnamon and ginger, and then add essence.

Lay out in heaps (desired size) on a wet cutting board or pastry board. Leave to cool.

Coconut harshé

1 coconut (diced)
1 lb sugar
1 small piece cinnamon
$\frac{1}{4}$ teaspoon nutmeg
1 teaspoon essence (cinnamon)
$\frac{1}{2}$ pint water

Method
Boil sugar in $\frac{1}{2}$ pint water together with prepared coconut and water, cinnamon and nutmeg stirring continuously until sugar is burnt. Add small quantities of water whilst stirring and continue until mixture becomes the consistency of syrup.

Remove from fire and pour into heaps (desired size) on to a greased board. Will harden when cool.

Unbreakables

2 lb sugar
1 cup water
food colouring

Method
Boil sugar and water to a thick syrup.
Add food colouring.

Pour on to a cutting board; then leave to cool, cut into desired shapes and sizes.

Peaceful living amongst fruit, flowers and coconut palms

Ginger 'cake'

2 oz green ginger (crushed)
2 cups sugar
1 cup water

Method
Boil sugar and water until crystals
form around saucepan. Add crushed
ginger or extract juice from ginger
and add to saucepan.

Remove from heat and beat until
mixture thickens. Pour on to a damp
board and allow to cool before
cutting into squares (or desired
shapes).

Chilli bibbi

1 cup dried corn
4 oz sugar

Method
Roast corn and grind. Sift. Add sugar,
mixing thoroughly. Put into paper
parcels.

Poiline (cashew nut sweet)

2 pints fresh cashew nuts
2 lb sugar
½ cup water

Method
Bring all ingredients to the boil. Boil
until crystals form around saucepan.

Remove from heat and beat until
mixture thickens. Pour into moulds
and allow to cool.

Peppermint sweet

2 cups sugar
1 cup water
peppermint essence

Method
Boil sugar and water until crystals
form around saucepan. Add
peppermint essence in desired
amount.

Remove from heat and beat until
mixture thickens. Pour on to a damp
board and allow to cool before
cutting into squares (or desired
shapes).

Jellies and jams

Golden apple jelly

golden apples (desired quantity)
sugar
water

Method
Select fruit that is not too ripe. Peel, wash and slice. Boil in just enough water to cover.

Strain off the liquid and combine it cup-for-cup with sugar. Boil until thick enough for jelly.

Pour into jars while still hot and leave to cool.

Guava jelly

guava (desired quantity)
sugar
water

Method
Select fruit that is not too ripe. Wash and cut in half, boil in just enough water to cover.

Strain off the liquid and combine it cup-for-cup with sugar. Boil until thick enough for jelly.

Pour into jars while still hot and leave to cool.

Cherry jam

cherries (desired quantity)
sugar
water

Method
For every pound of fruit prepare a syrup of 1 lb sugar to 2 cups water. Wash fruit and boil in prepared syrup until mixture reaches the consistency of jam.

Pour into jars while still hot and leave to cool.

Gooseberry jam

gooseberry (desired quantity)
sugar
water

Method
For every pound of fruit prepare a syrup of 1 lb sugar to 2 cups water. Wash fruit; then pour boiling water over it. Let fruit remain in water for about 5 minutes then drain (you may retain this water for making a drink).

Boil drained fruit in prepared syrup until mixture reaches the consistency of jam.

Pour into jars while still hot and leave to cool.

Breadfruit flower jam

12 breadfruit flowers
1 lb sugar
1 cup water

Method
Soak flowers in cold water until skin can easily be removed; then peel. Boil peeled flowers in water and drain – do this three times. After draining the third time squeeze water from flowers and slice.

Make syrup with sugar and water. Boil sliced flowers in syrup over low heat for about 15 minutes, or until syrup is absorbed; then bottle.

Note: see page 93 for Sweet potato jam

12

Beverages

Governor plum drink

4 cups ripe plums
peel of 1 green lime
small piece spice (cinnamon)
small piece of ginger (crushed)
5 cups water
1 lb sugar

Method
In a saucepan place 4 cups water; add plums, spice, lime peel and ginger. Boil for 30 minutes. Remove from heat; add last cup of water. Strain and leave to stand until cool. Sweeten to taste and bottle.
   Serve with ice.

Sorrel

2 pints dried sorrel
6 cloves
1 piece green ginger (crushed)
6 cups water
sugar, to taste

Method
Cut red petals from sorrel and put to boil with water, ginger and cloves. Boil for 20 minutes. Remove from heat and leave to stand overnight. Strain, sweeten to taste and bottle.
   Serve with ice.

Sea moss

$\frac{1}{2}$ oz sea moss
juice of 1 lime
$\frac{1}{4}$ teaspoon grated nutmeg
1 piece of cinnamon
4 cups of water
milk, as required
sugar, to taste

Method
Wash sea moss and soak in water overnight, then strain. In a saucepan boil together sea moss, water and the juice of the lime. Boil for 2 hours. When the moss is melted, strain: to every cup strained add $\frac{1}{2}$ cup milk, then put to boil with nutmeg and cinnamon. Once boiled, sweeten and remove from heat.
   Serve with ice.

99

Mauby

mauby bark
$\frac{1}{2}$ lime (optional)
water, as desired (approx 2 pints)
sugar

Method
Place mauby bark, water and lime in container and leave to stand for two days. Strain and sweeten to taste. Serve with ice.

or

Bring mauby bark to the boil in sufficient water. Leave to cool, then add lime juice. It be may be necessary to add more water to lessen bitterness. Add sugar to taste.

An old-time cocoa mill

*Cocoa pods. Cocoa beans and
a teeming cup of hot chocolate*

Cocoa

4 sticks cocoa
$\frac{1}{2}$ teaspoon nutmeg
1 small piece spice (cinnamon)
1 vanilla pod
small sprig anise
1 cup coconut milk
2 pints water
sugar, to taste

Method
Either grate or break up cocoa sticks.
Boil in $\frac{1}{2}$ pint water together with
nutmeg, vanilla and anise. When the
cocoa is melted add coconut milk and
remaining water. Taste and add sugar
if desired. Bring to the boil, then
remove from heat.

Serve either as a hot or cold
beverage.

Chaudo (egg-nog)

1 tablespoon brandy or *rum*
2 eggs
1 pint milk
4 tablespoons white sugar
$\frac{1}{2}$ teaspoon nutmeg
peel of 1 green lime

Method
Beat eggs together with sugar and
lime peel. In a saucepan bring milk to
the boil and pour over egg mixture
adding all other ingredients. Whisk
until frothy.

Serve hot or warm.

Floating island

3 eggs
1 pint milk
3 tablespoons sugar
1 tablespoon guava jelly
almond essence, to taste

Method
Warm milk in a saucepan and beat
with yolks of eggs, gradually adding
2 tablespoons sugar. Allow to cool
slightly before pouring into dish or
individual serving glasses. Top with
stiffly whisked egg whites to which
guava jelly and 1 tablespoon sugar
have been added.
Serve warm.

Sanguire

1 bottle unsweetened claret wine
2 pints water
2 oz spice
1 nutmeg (grated)
sugar, to taste

Method
Put water and spice to boil until the
water has reduced to 1 pint. Remove
from heat and leave to cool.
Add claret wine and sweeten to
taste. Pour into wine glasses and
sprinkle nutmeg on top.
Serve warm.

Anisette

1 pint proof rum
1 bundle anise
2 cups water
1 lb sugar

Method
Place anise and rum together in a
bottle and leave to stand for 3 days.
Make a syrup with water and
sugar. Add to the rum. Allow to cool,
then strain and bottle.
Serve with ice.

Milk cocktail

1 bottle rum
1 tin evaporated milk
1 tin condensed milk
grated rind of 1 lime
$\frac{1}{2}$ teaspoon grated nutmeg
glacé cherries
sugar, to taste

Method
Thoroughly mix together rum, evaporated milk, condensed milk, grated lime rind and nutmeg. Sweeten to taste. Place a cherry into each serving glass and pour mixture on top.

Serve with crushed ice.

Coconut cocktail

1 bottle white rum
1 tin evaporated milk
1 tin condensed milk
1 large coconut (grated)
$\frac{1}{2}$ teaspoon grated lime rind

sugar, if required
pineapple slices or lime slices
    (optional)

Method
Place coconut in muslin cloth (or gauze) and soak in warm water. Squeeze to extract milk from coconut, enough to make 1 pint milk. To this add rum, evaporated milk, condensed milk, and grated lime rind. Mix thoroughly, and sweeten to taste. Pour into serving glasses.

Garnish glass, if desired, with pineapple slice or lime slice. Serve with crushed ice.

Note: a quicker method would be to liquidise grated coconut in a blender and strain milk. Blend all ingredients with coconut milk and serve.

13

Non-traditionals

Pudding and pies

Corn Creole

1 sweet pepper
3 tablespoons olive oil
1 egg
$\frac{1}{2}$ cup corn meal
1 onion (sliced)
1 tin whole corn kernel
2 cups milk

Method
Mince sweet pepper and sauté in oil together with sliced onion. Add corn kernel; then stir in the beaten egg and milk. Bring almost to the boil, then remove from heat. Sift in corn meal. Allow to cool until mixture thickens.

Pour into a greased dish and bake in a low oven for 1 hour.

Breadfruit pudding

(Serves 6–8)
1 ripe breadfruit
8 oz sugar
1 teaspoon cinnamon
1 teaspoon grated nutmeg
1 teaspoon vanilla essence
1 teaspoon almond essence
2 teaspoons baking powder
1 egg
4 oz butter or margarine
$\frac{1}{2}$ cup milk
2 oz raisins
2 tablespoons rum
2 tablespoons flour

Method
Peel breadfruit, remove the centre of fruit and beat or blend the pulp until soft.

Cream sugar and butter for 10 minutes, then add pulp. Continue to cream for a further 15 minutes before adding the egg, essence and rum to the mixture. Beat thoroughly. Gradually add milk alternately with flour to which baking powder has been added.

Pour the mixture into a greased dish. Bake in moderate oven or until the pudding leaves the side of dish.

Breadfruit and sweetcorn pie

1 breadfruit
sweetcorn, as desired

Method
Peel breadfruit; boil in salted water
until tender, then blend or mash. Mix
in sweetcorn leaving some for the
topping. Pour mixture into a greased
dish and top with leftover corn.

Bake in a moderate oven for
30 minutes.

Creamed-breadfruit pie

1 ripe breadfruit
$\frac{1}{2}$ pint evaporated milk
2 oz margarine
1 tin peas and carrots
dash garlic salt
salt and pepper, to taste

breadcrumbs, as required

Method
Peel breadfruit and boil in salted
water. Mash or blend while still hot.

In a saucepan heat milk and
margarine; add salt and pepper. Beat
heated mixture into crushed
breadfruit until it is a creamy
consistency. Pour half of the mixture
into a greased dish. Arrange peas and
carrots over the mixture in the dish,
then sprinkle with garlic salt. Cover
with the remaining breadfruit mixture
and top with breadcrumbs.

Bake in a moderate oven for
15 minutes.

Pumpkin and coconut pudding

1 coconut (grated)
1 lb pumpkin (grated)
1 lb sweet potato (grated)
8 oz brown sugar
4 oz margarine
1 pint evaporated milk
6 eggs

Method
Mix together the coconut, pumpkin
and sweet potato. Now beat the
sugar and margarine well together
until light, then mix thoroughly with
the coconut, pumpkin and sweet
potato.

Whip milk and eggs together, add
to mixed ingredients. Stir until well
blended and pour into a buttered pan.

This mixture can either be baked
or steamed.

Coconut bread pudding

4 cups soaked bread
1 egg
2 cups milk
1 cup coconut (grated)
2 cups sugar
2 teaspoons vanilla essence
½ teaspoon nutmeg
1 teaspoon mixed spice
grated rind of 1 lime

butter, as required

Method
Squeeze all water out of bread and crush with a fork.

Make a custard with beaten egg and milk. Add to the crushed bread. Stir thoroughly. Add all other ingredients and stir well.

Set aside for 30 minutes, then pour into greased baking dish. Dot with butter and bake in a moderate oven.

Banana toad-in-the-hole

5 whole green bananas
(or 3 cups boiled and crushed banana)
¼ cup evaporated milk
½ cup celery (chopped)
¼ cup green pepper (chopped)
¼ teaspoon black pepper
1 teaspoon seasoning with salt
juice of ½ lime or lemon
4 eggs
1 pint water
salt, to taste
1 tablespoon margarine
1 tablespoon breadcrumbs
½ cup cheddar cheese (grated)

Method
Boil eggs until hard, shell, then set aside.

Peel green bananas and wash with water and lime. Place washed bananas in water with a pinch of salt; boil until soft. Strain and crush bananas while still hot. Setting the eggs, margarine, breadcrumbs and cheese aside, blend all the remaining ingredients with crushed banana until the texture is smooth.

Using margarine grease an oblong pie dish and spread the banana mixture on the bottom and sides of the dish. Place whole hard boiled eggs lengthwise to the dish letting them touch each other. Cover with mixture. Sprinkle the top with the remainder of the breadcrumbs and grated cheese.

Bake in a moderate oven until cheese is melted. Remove from dish when cool.

When sliced the egg will show in the middle of pie.

Dasheen cheese

2 or 3 small dasheens
6 oz cheese (grated)
1 pint milk
2 tablespoons margarine
2 tablespoons flour
1 onion (sliced)
salt and pepper, to taste

butter, as required

Method
Steam dasheen; then either dice or slice. Place in a greased dish.

Prepare a thin cheese sauce with all the other ingredients leaving 2 tablespoons grated cheese for topping. Pour prepared sauce over dasheen. Sprinkle with remaining cheese and dot with butter. Bake in a moderate oven.

Stuffing

Breadnut stuffing

2 lb breadnuts
2 small onions
3 sprigs fresh parsley
8 oz butter or margarine
2 cups biscuit crumbs
1 egg
$\frac{1}{2}$ cup evaporated milk
2 teaspoons garlic powder
$\frac{1}{8}$ teaspoon grated nutmeg
2 teaspoons seasoning salt
salt, to taste

Method
Boil breadnuts, then peel. Crush (or pound) breadnuts while still hot and set aside.

Chop onions and sauté in melted butter. Add crushed breadnut, stirring until thoroughly mixed. Beat egg and add to the mixture.

In a large bowl combine parsley, biscuit crumbs, garlic powder, grated nutmeg and seasoning salt. Add to the breadnut mixture. Gradually add milk to soften the mixture, salt to taste.

This quantity should stuff a 5 lb turkey.

Sauces

Banana sauce

onions, tomatoes, ketchup, water
   (quantity depends on how much
   sauce is desired)
a few drops Angostura Bitters
butter, as required
curry powder, to taste
bouquet garni
ripe bananas (sliced)
sugar, as required
salt and pepper, to taste

Method
Slice onions and tomatoes and sauté
in butter until tender. Add curry
powder to taste. Mix well. Add
bouquet garni, salt, pepper, ketchup
and Bitters. Using enough water to
cover ingredients, bring to the boil.
When the sauce is done, before
serving add sugar and slices of ripe
bananas.
   Serve with rice.

Cucumber sauce

cucumbers (quantity as desired)
$\frac{1}{2}$ cup vinegar
$\frac{1}{4}$ cup oil
1 teaspoon prepared mustard
pinch salt and pepper
sugar, to taste

Method
Score cucumbers lengthwise, or peel.
Cut into thin slices. Mix well all other
ingredients to make a dressing.
Marinate cucumber slices in dressing.
   Serve cold.

Sorrel sauce

1 lb sorrel sepals
2 pints water
1 lb sugar

Method
Wash sepals, add water and bring to
the boil in a heavy-bottomed
saucepan. Boil until liquid reduces to
1 pint, then add sugar and continue to
boil on low heat until the mixture
thickens. Cool and store in jars.
Note: Can be used as a substitute for
cranberry sauce as a complement to
ham or turkey.

Salads

Breadfruit salad

1 breadfruit
1 tin green peas or 1 cup fresh stewed
   pigeon peas
1 cup carrots (diced)
1 medium onion (chopped)
1 tablespoon parsley (chopped)
2 teaspoons vinegar
1 tablespoon vegetable oil
4 tablespoons mayonnaise
1 teaspoon mustard (optional)
1 teaspoon granulated sugar
salt, to taste

Method
Peel and steam breadfruit in a small amount of water. Dice when cool.

In a large bowl mix all ingredients making sure breadfruit is well coated with mayonnaise (if required use additional mayonnaise).

Serve cold.

Potato salad

2 lb potatoes (not sweet potato)
1 tin green peas or 1 cup fresh stewed
   pigeon peas
1 cup carrots (diced)
1 medium onion (chopped)
1 tablespoon parsley (chopped)
2 teaspoons vinegar
1 tablespoon vegetable oil
4 tablespoons mayonnaise
1 teaspoon mustard (optional)
1 teaspoon granulated sugar
salt, to taste

Method
Peel and boil potatoes until tender; dice when cool.

In a large bowl mix all ingredients making sure potato is well coated with mayonnaise (if required use additional mayonnaise).

Serve cold.

Banana salad

6 green bananas
2 eggs
1 tin green peas
2 tablespoons mayonnaise
1 onion (chopped)
1 lime
salt and pepper, to taste

Method
Peel bananas and wash with lime and water. Place in water with a pinch of salt and bring to the boil until cooked. Remove from heat, drain and allow to cool, then dice.

 Hard boil the eggs, shell and chop them.

 In a large bowl, mix the diced bananas, chopped eggs and all other ingredients.

 Serve cold with fried chicken or fried fish, and tossed green salad.

Dasheen salad

1 medium-sized dasheen
2 tablespoons olive oil
2 large heads chive (chopped)
1 tablespoon chopped parsley
salt and pepper

celery (chopped), as required

Method
Peel and wash dasheen thoroughly; put to boil in salted water. When cooked, cool and dice.

 In a bowl, mix together diced cooked dasheen with chopped chive and coat thoroughly with olive oil. Add salt and pepper to taste. Decorate with chopped celery.

 Serve cold with fried chicken or fried fish, and tossed green salad.

Note: For Lambie salad turn to page 57.

The author, aged five, in national dress

Glossary

Annatto or roucou or ochroe
Small reddish berries used by the Caribs as war-paint. The berries were also used to provide colouring in cooking. They were used extensively during the Second World War. Today they are still used by the Caribs, mainly as a colourant in cooking.

Broth
Known as 'Fish Soup' in some Caribbean Islands but is the local name given to a thin soup or 'One-pot' made of ground provisions with meat or fish which may be smoked, salted or fresh.

Boucan
Another name for a *galta*.

Bouquet garni
A bundle of fresh herbs tied together (chive, parsley, thyme).

Callalou
The name given to a thick soup, the chief ingredient being the callalou leaves, or more popularly made with the unopened leaves of the dasheen or tannia plant. It is also made with the uncultivated spinach leaves known as *Zepina* (amaranthus).

Cassareep
The juice of boiled-down cassava water. The early Caribs used it as a form of food preservation.

Cassava
Also known as manioc, was the main staple of the Caribs. The flour from the grated, starchy tuber is used either to make cassava bread, or more popularly as 'Farine' (see Farine, page 73).

Christophine
A pear-shaped, squash-like vegetable – green or white skinned – with firm flesh surrounding a small stone (seed).

Coconut milk
Juice extracted from grated, dry coconut by soaking the grated nut in a bowl of warm water and leaving it to soak for 30 minutes; then squeezing through a sieve or cloth. The milky liquid is called coconut milk and the quantity of milk extracted depends on the amount of water used.

Crapaud
A large, edible frog known as mountain chicken. Considered a delicacy, it is Dominica's national dish. It is an endangered species and can only be caught at certain periods of the year.

Creole (*or* Kweyol)
The french patois spoken by most Dominicans.

Chaudo
The Creole name given to Egg-nog.

Coubouillon
Plain, boiled fish.

Daub
Method of stewing meat, fish or shell-fish.

Dasheen
Round, dark-brown root crop. When peeled has a white flesh which may appear to be dark grey when cooked.

Farine
Grated cassava parched dry. Popularly used as a dish with mashed avocado or peas, or as a cereal with milk.

Galta
A stand erected above a fireplace to accommodate meat or fish to be smoked. This stand is usually made of wattle sticks.

Ground provisions
The name given to root crops such as cassava, dasheen, eddoes, etc.

Lele
A stick with three or four small handles protruding from the end, resembling the foot of a chicken. This stick is used for stirring or swizzling. Popularly used to whisk Chaudo (Egg-nog) and Floating Island.

Marinade
A liquid used for seasoning by soaking. Usually a mixture of wine, oil and seasonings. This is also a method of tenderising the meats.

Marinate
To cook in a marinade in order to soften and add flavour.

Pigeon-peas
The different varieties of the most common are grown in a long pod about the length of a finger. The pods are mostly green coloured with the peas a lighter shade of green. When dried, the peas are brown in colour. Pigeon-peas can be stewed or cooked together with rice. Plentiful for harvest during the months of December–February they are therefore a popular dish at Christmas.

Pound
To soften by using a pestle and mortar.

Skim
To remove foam, fat, or solid substances from the surfaces of a cooking mixture.

Bibliography

Atwood, Thomas, *The History of the Island of Dominica*, Frank Cass & Co. Ltd, London, 1971

Beattie, John, *Other Cultures*, Routledge & Kegan Paul, London, 1966

Benedict, Ruth, *Patterns of Culture*, New American Library, Houghlin Mifflin, 1993

Chuto, James, and Martin, W.L., *A Kitchen in Corfu*, New Amsterdam Books, New York, 1987

Dorje, Rinjing, *Food in Tibetan Life*, Prospect Books, London, 1985

Francy, Pierre, *New York Times – Sixty Minute Gourmet*, Fawcett Random House, Columbine, New York, 1979

Gray, Patience, *Honey From a Weed: Fasting and Feasting in Tuscany, Catalonia, the Cyclades and Apulia*, Harper & Row, London, 1986

Grey, Winnifred, *Carribean Cookery*, Collins, London

Harris, Dunstan, *Island Cooking: Recipes from the Caribbean*, The Crossing Press, Freedom, California, 95019, 1990

Henderson, T.H., 'Communication', Cajanus: Vol 6, No. 3, July–September 1973, Caribbean Food and Nutrition Institute, University of the West Indies, P O Box 40, Kingston 7, Jamaica

Hilchoy, Florence, *Heirloom Recipes*, Nova Scotia Department of Agriculture & Marketing, 1967

Honychurch, Lennox, *Dominica, Isle of Adventure*, McMillan Silvestein Ltd., Macmillan Caribbean, London and Basingstoke, 1991

Homma, Gaku, *The Folk Art of Japanese Country Cooking*, Colorado North Atlantic Books, Berkeley, California, 1991

Horowitz, Michael, M., *Peoples of Culture of the Caribbean*, Natural History Press, New York Garden City, 1971

Jelliffe, D.B., Cajanus: Vol. 6, No. 2, 1973

Leonard, Peter, *Sociology in Social Work*, Routledge & Kegan Paul, 1966

Miller, Elsa, *Caribbean Cookbook, Using the Foods we Grow*, Kingston Publishers Ltd, 1A Norwood Avenue, Kingston 5, Jamaica, 1979

Ragatz, L.J., *The Fall of the Planter Class in the British Caribbean, 1763–1883*, Octagon Books, New York, 1928

Taylor, Douglas, *Aspects of Dominican History*, Government of Dominica, Government Printing, 1967

Trovesicle, Lake, *Rural Native Heritage Cookbook; The Gathering* Vol. 1, Native Women's Association

Williams, R. Omosunlola, *Miss Williams' Cooking Book*, Longmans, Green & Co., London, 1957

Index